KU-507-389

PRAYER

Abhishiktananda

HENRI LE SAUX, O.S.B.

LONDON

S·P·C·K

First published 1967
by I.S.P.C.K.
P.O. Box 1585
Delhi
Reprinted 1969

Revised edition 1972
Second impression 1972
Third impression (with corrections) 1974
Published by S.P.C.K.
Holy Trinity Church
Marylebone Road
London NW1 4DU

Made and printed in Great Britain by
The Talbot Press, Saffron Walden, Essex

SBN 281 02663 7

CONTENTS

1. THE HOLY PRESENCE   1

2. A MYSTERY OF FAITH   6

3. THE UNIVERSAL THEOPHANY   13

4. THE CALL WITHIN   20

5. GOD'S REST   27

6. THE OUTER COURTS   35

7. SILENCE AND YOGA   39

8. THE WORD OF GOD   45

9. THE PRAYER OF THE NAME   51

10. OM! ABBA!   59

NOTES   65

1

THE HOLY PRESENCE

Jesus commanded his disciples to pray always. He himself was constantly in prayer, remembering the name of the Father at all times and spending the nights, according to St Luke, "in prayer to God" (Luke 6.12). To remain awake, to watch and pray, was his ceaseless counsel, so that the disciples might always be ready for his coming (Mark 13.33). After the Master, St Paul gives the same teaching to the Churches: "Pray constantly" (1 Thess. 5.17); "Pray at all times in the Spirit with all prayer and supplication. To that end keep alert with all perseverance" (Eph. 6.18).

Prayer is not a part-time occupation for any of Christ's disciples—nor indeed is it so for any truly religious man. There are not two classes of Christians, some whose whole life should be devoted to prayer—whom we might call "full-time contemplatives"—and others whose life is to be engaged in various activities, in family or society, or even in studying and preaching the word of God, and who therefore can only be "part-time" contemplatives.

Indeed there are no "part-time contemplatives", any more than there are part-time Christians or part-time men. From the day when we begin to believe in Christ and to acknowledge him as our Lord, there is not a single moment of our time—waking, sleeping, walking, sitting, working, teaching, eating, playing,—which is not marked by the claim of God upon us and which has not to be lived in the name of Jesus, under the inspiration of the Holy Spirit, to the glory of the Father.

To live in constant prayer, to lead a contemplative life, is nothing else than to live in the actual presence of God. Every man indeed, by the very fact that he exists, is already in the

1

presence of God. This is especially true of the Christian man, who has been called to know the ultimate secrets of divine life, since by his baptism he has become a sharer in the divine sonship of Jesus, his Master.

To live in the presence of God should be as natural for a Christian as to breathe the air which surrounds him. Furthermore, to live consciously and worthily in this presence should never have for him even the appearance of a duty which he is bound to perform in obedience to some external law. No, for him to live in the presence of the Almighty is a birthright; it is the deepest aspiration of his nature, it is the spontaneous expression of his love for the Lord when he knows that he is a child of God.

God is always present to us. There is no time and no place in our daily life or occupations in which God is not present to us; there are not even certain times or occupations in which God is more present to us or less present to us. God is always the same, the Almighty, the Infinite, the Eternal. He does not change, neither does he "come" or "go" from one place to another. Everywhere and always he is, he is himself in his fulness; there is no sense in which he can be more "here" or less "there", since he is indivisible. In truth it is to himself alone that God is ever present. From eternity he is for himself and in himself. He enjoys for ever the unspeakable bliss of his Presence to himself, the Presence of the Father to the Son and of the Son to the Father, and the mutual Presence of both to the Holy Spirit. This mystery is revealed to us by Jesus himself, out of his experience as Son of God (John 14.10, 11, 16; 15.10, 26; 16.13, 14; 17.5, 22-4).

Creation is simply the communication of this Presence, this mysterious life of God in himself. Everything that exists, every being that lives and thinks, does so by sharing in his being, his divine life and self-awareness. It is from and through this very Presence of God to himself that all creatures exist, that living creatures are born and grow, that man is aware of himself, and finally becomes an individual being, endowed with a personal call and vocation for time and eternity.

Man, alone among creatures, has the privilege of being aware

2

of this Presence and of being called to reciprocate it; that is, he is called to be present to God as God is present to him, in the way in which, within the Blessed Trinity, the Son of God is eternally present to the Father as the Father is present to him. Did not Jesus assure us that our relationship with him, and through him with the Father, is actually modelled on his own relationship with the Father, "I know my own and my own know me, as the Father knows me and I know the Father" (John 10.14-15); ". . . . as thou, Father, art in me and I in thee, (I pray) that they also may be one in us . . . . that they may be one even as we are one. I in them and thou in me, that they may become perfectly one . . . ." (John 17.21-3).

The life of prayer, the life of contemplation, is simply to realize God's Presence to us. It is therefore not a special way of life reserved for those few individuals who are called to get away from the world and to dwell in the deserts. Contemplation and prayer ought to be the very breath of every disciple of Christ.

But there remains the problem which troubles so many people: How can I remain always in prayer? There is even the preliminary question: How can I pray at all? We wonder, however, whether such problems do not arise mainly from the wrong conceptions of prayer that men generally have, and perhaps, even more basically, from the wrong conceptions they too often have of the mystery of God.

Most people actually imagine that in order to pray, and especially, in order to find themselves in the Presence of God, they have to stop their minds from thinking of any creature whatsoever, and instead to form some mental picture or idea of God, or rather about God, and then to busy themselves mentally with that image or that concept. Yet is it not a fact that no image or idea which we may form of God is God himself, but remains inevitably and for ever simply *what we think of God?*

It is just the same with our ideas of God as it is with statues and icons which many Christians like to have in their churches or in their houses. A crucifix, or a picture of Christ, is not Christ himself; nor are icons of saints identical with the saints they represent. Their immediate function is to catch the eyes and hold

3

the attention of the worshippers, which are always too inclined to run away towards worldly and temporal things, and to refresh their minds with the remembrance of the saints or of the Lord. It is true that they may also be something more than that, at least when they have been ritually blessed and consecrated; the faithful are then fully authorized to believe piously that they communicate some halo of the divine presence.

The same applies to the mental images and ideas of God which we form when we study or meditate. They are signs pointing to the Reality they represent, but they are for ever unable to comprehend that reality, which stands in its aloneness far beyond the reach of any conception or imagination of man.

When indeed those images and ideas come to us from the divine revelation, or at least arise from the deep spiritual experience of sages and saints—being no mere inventions of man, as were the idols derided by the Prophets—they of themselves lead us effectively and directly into the Presence of God and make us become more aware of his divine Reality. However, even so we must never forget that they remain always on the level of signs. The day in which we attempt to identify them with the Reality they become simply idols; and mental idols are no less vanity and nothingness than stone or metal ones. The most perfect prayer necessarily makes use of signs, because the human mind has been created such by God, but it makes use of them with full liberty and sovereignty and it tends always towards the *Beyond* where alone Reality abides in the unfathomable silence of the Godhead.

Jesus, in the course of a few years, gave his *darshan*[1] freely to his disciples and readily allowed himself to be seen by crowds of his contemporaries. Yet that external *darshan* of himself which he gave through eyes, ears, and touch, was not to last for ever. The real and decisive knowledge of Jesus was to be received from the Holy Spirit alone. Flesh and blood do not lead far, they are unable to possess the kingdom (1 Cor. 15.50); "It is the Spirit that gives life, the flesh is of no avail" (John 6.63); "For the Spirit searches everything, even the depths of God" (1 Cor. 2.10). He alone can give us the real *darshan* of the one who dwells in the bosom of the Father (John 1.18). For that reason

4

Jesus used to tell his own: "It is to your advantage that I go away, for if I do not go away the Counsellor will not come to you . . . ."), and "He will guide you into all the truth" (John 16.7, 13, etc.). Then Jesus left the world in his bodily presence. On the day of the Ascension he disappeared behind the clouds and vanished from the eyes of his disciples and of his mother. Yet who could say that Mary and the Apostles lost anything when their eyes of flesh were no longer able to contemplate the visage of Jesus, their ears to hear his voice, their hands to touch him, their bodies to rejoice in his embrace? The grace of Pentecost was far greater than any that Jesus could have conferred on his own while living among them in his mortal body. Such was his ultimate Transfiguration, of which the first one, on Mount Tabor, was only a kind of announcement and prefiguraion.

The main purpose of the foregoing remarks is to make it clearly understood that the presence of the Lord to us and our presence to him—rather, our awareness of him being here—have nothing to do with any particular working of our senses or minds.

Yet there are still too many forms of prayer in use among Christians which are liable to mislead the faithful; for instance, the first words of the morning prayer in some not-so-old catechisms: "Let us put ourselves in the presence of God and adore him!"—as if it were possible for anyone to place himself or to remain *outside* the presence of God! To be out of the divine Presence would indeed mean death, or rather the complete annihilation or extinction of man's very being.

Do we say: "Let us first think of the air which surrounds us and then breathe?" Willingly, unwillingly, consciously, unconsciously, we breathe and go on breathing; continuously, too, air is entering our lungs. So it is also with the divine Presence which is more essential to our life, to our very being, than the air itself which we breathe.

2

A MYSTERY OF FAITH

Entrance into prayer is an act of faith. By saying that, we mean not only that, when we think of God, we have to believe that he is, but that we believe he is everywhere, he is in everything, he is the origin and the source of everything, the end and the consummation to which all creatures are moving.

Praying is simply believing that we are living in the mystery of God, that we are encompassed by that mystery, that we are really plunged into and immersed in it—"in him we live and move and have our being" (Acts 17.28)—that the mystery of God in its fulness is both inside and outside us, within and without, like the air which surrounds us and penetrates into the tiniest hollows of our lungs.

Now, what do we mean by the "mystery of God"? It is not simply the existence of some High Power or High Personage abiding far above, beyond the skies. It is in reality the very mystery of the divine Life, welling up eternally in the Father and eternally expanding itself in the processions of the Son and of the Holy Spirit.

The mystery of God is nothing else than the eternal call of the Father to the Son, the Second Person of the Blessed Trinity: "Thou art my beloved Son" (Mark 1.11; Ps. 2.7), and the eternal answer of the Son to the Father: "Abba, Pater. Thou, my Father" (Rom. 8.15; Gal. 4.5)—the prayer which was always on the lips of Jesus and in his heart when he was dwelling as a mortal amongst us mortals, and which he is still addressing to the Father in heaven, the summing up, as it were, of his love, his sacrifice, and of his unending intercession.

The divine life is also the pervading Presence of the Holy Spirit in everything. The Holy Spirit is in us, as he is in God, the mystery of unity, of non-duality.[1] He is in us, welling up from the Father and dwelling in us, in the innermost recesses of our hearts, "more intimate to us even than we are intimate to ourselves" (St Augustine), and making us inwardly present also to each other, in the same way as the Son and the Father really abide in each other.

The Spirit is present in the whole creation, preparing for the final gathering up of all into Christ, the Son. He is present in the core of each being, in the heart of each man, as a ceaseless call and longing, as an unquenchable thirst for this unity and *koinonia*.[2] In him the elect already possess and enjoy the *things-to-come*, for all things to come are already present in the eternity of God, and he who possesses the Spirit possesses everything that belongs to the Father and the Son.

Christian life is simply a life of faith.[3] This life of faith takes seriously the divine status to which we have been raised by our baptism—for by baptism we have become "partakers of the divine nature" (2 Pet. 1.4); it also heeds the call which the Holy Spirit unceasingly addresses to the heart of each man: "Come to the Father", as the great bishop and martyr Ignatius[4] expressed it so beautifully in his letter to the Romans (7.2).

Christian life is a life of faith from the beginning to the end, reaching to the minutest details of man's existence. "The righteous shall live by his faith", as St Paul asserts (Rom. 1.18), confirming the words of the prophet Habakkuk (Hab. 2.4), but with a meaning renewed and amplified by his own experience of Christ. When faith is deep—or rather, is simply true—there is no real problem in Christian existence. Difficulties which appear insuperable are overcome by faith—"In all these things we are more than conquerors through him who loved us" (Rom. 8.37; cp. Heb. 11). That does not mean that there is no place in the Christian life for passion and sacrifice. Christian life, on the contrary, is bound to be a participation in the cross of Jesus. But faith is precisely that divine force which took Jesus from Gethsemane up to the Resurrection. It is in the power of faith that the Christian overcomes all obstacles, obstacles arising from himself as well as obstacles arising from the world or from the

devil—" . . . . for he endured as seeing him who is invisible"
(Heb. 11.27).

"Where there is love, there is no toil" (*Ubi amatur non laboratur*), to quote St Augustine again. For the one who has faith, life presents no really insoluble problems. In all that he does on earth he is aware of the divine Presence, he is making a loving response to the call addressed to him by the Father; or rather, he is allowing the Holy Spirit to realize in him the work of love which God is expecting from him.

The Christian is not faced with a set of particular problems; for instance, how to love God, how to love and serve his neighbour, how to be disinterested and patient, how to put into practice the commandments of the Lord, and so forth. For it is not out of duty that we have to accomplish all those things, still less out of fear, as was the case under the old Covenant. In the New Testament, there is no place for law or slavish obedience, as St Paul takes so much trouble to explain. From Pentecost onwards, the law is the Spirit himself who dwells in us, who acts in us (Rom. 8), who transforms the whole life of Jesus' disciples —their life in their bodies and in their minds and in their social relations—into the life of the Son of God, Jesus, the first-born of creation and the first-risen from the dead (Col. 1.5, 18).

Faith, in short, is the coming face to face of man with God, the awareness of the divine Presence. Now, when we speak of this awareness we do not at all mean any kind of sensible or psychological awareness, in the manner, for instance, in which we are aware of the sun, or of the heat or light which come from it, or even of the mental processes which are at work in our minds during our waking hours. The awareness of faith is something both more real and much deeper. It takes place at the very centre of our awareness of ourselves, behind and beyond everything of which we are or might be conscious.

Faith is "of the invisible", as is explained so powerfully in the eleventh chapter of the letter to the Hebrews. And here the word *invisible* applies to what is beyond the range of mind as well as to what lies beyond the range of our external senses. God is invisible. Man cannot see him and remain alive, declare the Scriptures (Exod. 33.21). "Truly thou art a God who hidest thyself", confesses the prophet Isaiah (Isa. 45.15). Yet God is not hidden in the sense that he hides himself from us or deliberately withdraws his Presence from us. God does not move; all "approaching" or "departing" attributed to God in the Bible are only ways of conveying to us symbolically our own relationship with him in time, and our own "going to" him or "withdrawing from" him, as it were. Further, God is a loving Father, whose most earnest desire is to draw his children as close to himself as possible.

If God is hidden, it is because he is out of the reach of our senses or imagination, even of our mental perceptions. God and the world do not form a unity within the grasp of thought, as was generally supposed by the Greek philosophers—a belief which would reduce him to an object within the range of our minds. "He does not in any sense belong to the world of objects about which man orients himself through thought."[5] It is true that our reason can get at least some glimpse of his existence, and we learn even more about him through the revealed Scriptures; yet he remains always beyond any conceptual knowledge that man can have of him.

God loves us too much to allow us to be satisfied and contented with mere images or signs of his Presence, like the material icons that we see or the mental concepts of him that we form with our intelligence. It is to his most secret and hidden abode—symbolized by the clouds which covered Mount Sinai or enveloped Jesus at his Ascension—that God calls his beloved children. The words of Jesus in the Gospel exactly express the Father's will: "Father, I desire that they also . . . may be with me where I am" (John 17.24). Children have a birth-right to the dwelling-place of their Father. The mission on earth of Jesus, the eternal Son, was to call his brothers and to take them with himself to the very place of their heritage, the bosom of the Father. He came into this world to make it possible for us men also to become sons of the living God (John 1.12).

Faith is the only way of penetrating the hidden abode of God —in the highest heaven as well as in the deepest centre of our hearts.[6] Faith alone can take us beyond anything capable of being seen by the eye, heard by the ear, uttered by the tongue, thought of by the intellect—and we know from the Apostle Paul that the things prepared by God for those who love him are indeed unseen by the eye, unheard by the ear, and have never entered into the heart of man (1 Cor. 2.9).[7] Faith alone can introduce us to the ultimate mystery of God and also of ourselves, to the place where is revealed to each one of us the new name (Rev. 3.17) by which he is called by God in the eternal secret of his love. It is really in the secret utterance and hearing of that name that God's elect reach the bosom of their Father, and do so when they find him in the most secret place of their own hearts.

Faith is to be aware of the mystery of God—of the mystery of God in himself first, but also of that same mystery in which he manifests himself in all things up to the furthest limits of the universe.

Truly there is nothing in this universe, or indeed in the whole creation, which is not in itself a revelation, a manifestation of God to man. For in creating man God endowed him with intelligence so that he might understand this revelation and respond to this manifestation with faith and love. Does not St Paul in the first chapter of his letter to the Romans say that God is to be known through "the things that have been made" (Rom. 1.20), i.e., through the universe? Paul even speaks with the utmost severity, in the same passage, of those Gentiles who chose to ignore the manifestations of God's presence in his creation. How much more will his words condemn those Christians who live virtually without acknowledging it—and yet it is they above all who have the immense privilege of knowing the secrets and receiving the promises which kings and prophets of old were so eager to know and yet were unable to see or to hear (Luke 10.33)?

As we have already said, faith is not merely a part of Christian life. Faith and prayer are not the part-time occupation of men who at other times are engaged in quite other "occupations". Faith stands on a different plane from all other activities of man, material as well as intellectual. It does not compete with any of them; it is not to be compared in importance with any of them. Rather it encompasses all our activities, it penetrates all of them, it wholly transforms and renews them. Thus transformed by faith our activities find their ultimate significance in manifesting the spiritual destiny of each individual and of all mankind; for all men are called to contribute to the never-ending growth of the mystical Body of Christ on earth (Eph. 2.21; Col. 2.19) and to the completion of his Pleroma[8] (Eph. 3.19—4.13).

Faith, prayer, and contemplation are the internal realities underlying the external activities of the disciple of Jesus. They authenticate them and give them their supernatural value. The Christian man indeed is the one *who knows*, the one whose eyes have been opened to the divine Splendour, in whose heart has shined "the light of the knowledge of the glory of God in the face of Jesus Christ" (2 Cor. 4.6).

Faith, prayer, and contemplation are in reality the simple acknowledgement of the presence of the Spirit in everything, everywhere and at every moment. Faith and prayer are the realization that everything takes its origin in the eternal love of the Father; that it is held in being in the lordship of Christ—by whom everything has been made (John 1.3; Col. 1.16) and in whom everything subsists (Col. 1.17); and that it is impelled by the mysterious and intimate motion of the Spirit.

There is no single moment and no single act in a really Christian life which is not faith, prayer, and contemplation. This is the very breath of his regenerate soul. He breathes in the Spirit, as it were, as he breathes in the encompassing air to fill up his lungs—since the Spirit is present in the entire universe (Wisd. 1. 7). He also breathes out the Spirit, for the Spirit is present in him and the Spirit wants to blow forth through him and to vitalize the earth (John 7.37-8).

"The wind blows where it wills", Jesus said in St John (3.8), and man does not know "whence it comes or whither it goes". Indeed is it not above all from the hearts of saints that the wind of the Spirit breathes upon our world? And is it not towards the final communion of saints, in the heart of God, that he is moving and taking up everything in his movement? Is not the Spirit, in fact, that strong wind which began to stir the world on

11

the day of Pentecost? He seizes everything on earth, every particle of matter, every manifestation of life, every human perception and thought, every event in the life of individuals as well as of mankind at large, so as to bring all of them to their consummation in Christ at the end of time? The end will be, as St Paul expresses it, when the Lord will recapitulate all things, that is, gather them together under himself and sum them up in himself (Eph. 1.10). Then he will make the final oblation to the Father (1 Cor. 15.28), God being then and for ever all in all, and time having passed into eternity.

3

THE UNIVERSAL THEOPHANY

Prayer is not an escape from the work that God has entrusted to men during man's stay on earth. Man has indeed to collaborate with God in the process of the evolution of the universe; he has to serve God in the person of God's children living here below, he has to develop his own mind for the service of God and of his neighbours; he has to fulfil many duties, family, social or religious. But none of these activities is really profane in the strict sense of the term, because all that man is or does falls within the mystery of God and finds its place in the ceaseless growth of Christ into his Pleroma. Even though man is often forgetful of this fact, even though he sins, he cannot in the last resort place himself outside the mystery of God. Man sins when of set purpose he directs his action exclusively towards his own petty self, and, as it were, attempts to hold up at himself the stream of things and events on their way to God. It is precisely this which makes sin so hateful and unnatural. And yet even sin cannot check the design of God, for nothing mortal can thwart the working of the Spirit.

Still less is there anything really profane in the life of a redeemed man. As is said in the Scriptures, he has been taken up into the holiness of God: "You shall be holy; for I the Lord your God am holy" (Lev. 19.2); "You are a people holy to the Lord your God" (Deut. 7.6).

A Christian is no less a Christian when he attends to the needs of his body than when he sits or kneels in the church, singing the praises of the Lord or sharing in the eucharistic banquet. His whole life is filled with the divine Presence.

The Presence is always shining on us as the sun is shining on the earth from on high in the sky. At times we lift up our eyes to the sun and contemplate it directly in its brightness. But even when we turn away and look towards the objects on the surface of the earth, it is still the sun which gives them all those colours which enable us to see them, to distinguish and to recognize them. Even at night, when the sun has disappeared behind the horizon, it is still the sun that gives light and splendour to the moon which, by that time, has taken its place in the heavens. Moreover, even the clouds which at times hide the sun can only be seen by us because they are all penetrated by its light.

Prayer is to see God in any man, or in any creature with which we come in contact.

God has no form. He is beyond every form. Precisely for that reason he can reveal and manifest himself under any form. Nothing "comprehends" him, but he shines through everything and makes himself known in everything. No form may be considered unworthy to be his sign, for there is really no form at all which could worthily signify him.

Each man who comes to me on the path of my life is a manifestation of God to me. That is because that man *is*—as God *is*—and depends on, and shares in, God's being; because that man is aware of himself—as God is aware of himself—and depends on and shares in the divine awareness and knowledge. Every man indeed is called to enjoy face to face the vision of the living God. He is loved by the Father in heaven with a particular and definite love; and I cannot forget that the Father who is in heaven and who loves that man is the one who dwells in the centre of my soul as in his own personal abode. Furthermore every man is eternally called by a special *Thou* and a special name, known only to him and to the One who called him (Rev. 2.17); he will learn that name at the end of his pilgrimage, and called by that name he will enjoy for ever the glory and the intimacy of the divine Presence.

It does not mean that this man who comes across my path, whatever he may be in human eyes, will necessarily be endowed with all the precious qualities we like to attribute to God. Do we ourselves indeed so perfectly mirror the Lord in our minds, in our bodies, in all our behaviour? The urgent need is that my encounter with that man, in that very place, at that very moment

14

should bring out more brightly, more manifestly, the image of God, should unveil his secret mystery, both in him and in me. It is really in such meetings, in the communion of men with each other, that God manifests himself and reveals his secret of love. The life of the Blessed Trinity is a mystery of communion, of "encounter", of coming together, of being face to face in the unity of the Holy Spirit. God is everywhere, God alone is everywhere both hidden and unveiled in his manifestation: it is God who gives, God who receives, God who approaches, God who is approached, God who loves, God who is loved.

It is God, or more precisely, God incarnate, Christ Jesus the unique Lord, who is coming to me in the form of that other man. On the day of his Resurrection Jesus presented himself under unexpected forms to the eyes of Mary Magdalene, of the Apostles, and of the pilgrims to Emmaus, so as to teach them to recognize him under any form, and in any dress in which he might choose to appear. In the form of that man who stands in front of me—no matter whether he is about to bow before me or to strike me—it is Christ who wants to grow in him and in me together, who wants, through this very encounter, to make his Church brighter, his Pleroma fuller. It is God who comes to me, in the guise of this man, so that I may help this man through my love, my respect, my service, to draw out of himself the possibilities of divine life which lie hid in his nature.

Such a man may be coarse, rude, ugly, wicked. I may have to avoid too close contact with him, not to be hurt or maimed in my mind or body. I may have to threaten him, to rebuke him, I may have to claim what is due from him. Yet I can never forget that there is always in him a spark at least of divine love; I can never forget that, if this man is repulsive or wicked, it is not only his fault but also the fault of a society which does not accept him with love, not only his sin, but also the sin of his brothers—one of whom I am. I cannot but adore in him the countenance of the Lord—marred by the blood, the dust, and the spittle—the countenance of the Lord who is waiting for a Veronica![1] God needs, so to speak, my respect and my love for that man, in order to bring out of him the love of which he is capable. That is indeed the precise theology that underlies the

15

theory and practice of non-violence; to show such a love to the so-called foe, that the warmth and the fire of this love may in the end kindle the love which is dormant within him, deeply buried perhaps under mountains of egoism.

There is no need to describe here in detail the various ways of meeting God in the daily meetings of man with man in all the possible circumstances of life. It is faith, above all, which has to be always awake and alert. Faith itself will project its own light on all those circumstances and will dictate to the Christian the right attitude to have and the right action to take in each encounter.[2] Is not faith a fruit of the Spirit, as St Paul explained to the churches of Galatia (Gal. 5.22)? "Where the Spirit of the Lord is, there is freedom" (2 Cor. 3.17)—that is, freedom from all our egoism, from all the mean desires and attachments which prevent our own spirits from being lifted up by the Spirit present in us, and from soaring with him to the highest heavens of God, where everything is seen in its true condition and judged at its true value.

A few examples will be sufficient to start the train of our thoughts about this.

For the man whose calling in this world is, for instance, to teach and to educate others, prayer will be to see in his children and pupils the mystery of God, which is waiting, as it were, to be brought forth. For him, prayer is to help children to grow up in the knowledge of creation (including all the sciences of earth and of man), as the work of a loving God, to admire its marvels, and to praise the Lord for it; to help them to grow also in the knowledge of themselves, in the awareness of their inner soul, so that they discover deep within themselves the privileged place where God himself is waiting for them.

For him who is called to be a doctor or a nurse, prayer is, first of all, to nurse and doctor the sick, to bring back their bodies and minds to a state in which they will be again service-able instruments in the hands of their Creator, and also to help them to make the best spiritual use of their actual condition with patience and joy.

For those who are called to lead others in the social and

16

political sphere, prayer is the service which they do for their brothers, so that they may lead a life which more and more reflects their dignity as men and as the children of God, and also may direct their thoughts and actions in harmony towards the building up of the Body of Christ.

Prayer is the meeting of husband and wife in their whole life lived in common, including the most intimate act of their being together; it is the meeting of parents with their children, of the employer with the worker, of the merchant with the customer, the clerk with the inquirer, the bus driver with the passenger, and so on.

Prayer is the smile, the look of the eyes which conveys to any other man the greetings of a heart, which tells him, unknown as he may be and met by chance in a public place or vehicle, that he is not really a stranger, but is recognized and loved as a brother.

Prayer is the act of faith which springs up from the heart of a Christian man every time his eyes meet other men's eyes, his ears hear other men's voices, his body approaches or touches other men's bodies. All such external contacts aim, in the divine plan, at awakening the internal contact, the contact of souls, deep within the heart, and kindling love—that love which is the very life of God, Father, Son, and Holy Spirit.[3]

Every event in our life is meant to arouse in us an act of faith, of prayer, of contemplation. Anything, whatever happens, forms part of God's plan for the consummation of all in Christ. Yet prayer does not mean speculating about events and trying to understand how they manage actually to fit into the plan of God, how they serve the purpose of gathering up and fulfilling all in Christ. Prayer is rather a simple act of faith which, before any explanation rises in the mind, bows and adores the mystery of God: *"Ita, Pater"*,—"Yea, Father, for such was thy gracious will" (Matt. 11.26).

As Jesus says in the same passage of St Matthew, the kingdom of heaven is actually hidden from the wise and prudent of this world, even from many who proclaim themselves spiritual. They are too rich (Mark 10.22) to accept the constant gift of God, they are too intelligent to say with the *babes* (Matt. 11.25) "Yea, Father", and above all to say it, not with so-called resignation or acceptance under compulsion, but with the same joy which was prompted in the heart of Jesus by his discovering in everything the love of the Father.

For him who has faith everything comes from the Father and everything leads to the Father. Health, sickness, wealth, poverty, success, failure, and so on, are only manifestations of the holy will of God. After all, was the Father showing less love to his beloved Son Jesus, when he allowed him to be condemned and crucified by Pilate and the soldiers, than when he gave him to Mary to be fed and fondled by her?

It is an act of prayer and contemplation to look at the sun, at the stars, at the sky, when faith reveals in them the presence and love of the Creator, since through them he prepared the earth to be the cradle of mankind and the place of the Incarnation. Is it not through the sun particularly, through its light and heat, that life was made possible here below for the children of the Father, and especially for his first-born, the Lord Jesus, who blessed the sun for ever with his divine glance?[4]

To look with eyes enlightened by faith at trees and plants, at fruits and flowers, at birds and animals—all of them created by the Father to help and serve us and to be used by us in our ascent towards him—is also nothing less than prayer and contemplation. There is indeed nothing in the world whose impact on our senses should not blossom into prayer, when looked at with the eyes of faith, with the eyes of Jesus, the one who knows everything "in the Father". It could even be said that through our eyes and all our senses it is God himself who is looking at his own creation and taking his delight in it, who sees that it is all good (Gen. 1.9ff).

To pray without ceasing is not so much consciously to *think* of God, as to act continuously under the guidance of the Spirit; it is to live and act "in Christ" (Gal. 2.20) or rather, to allow Jesus to live freely in us his life as the Son of God. It is to be attentive to the Father who comes to us by any path he may choose.[5] It is to hear in all creatures and every event the call which comes to us from the eternity of God, the *Thou* which the

18

Father addresses mysteriously to each one of us within the *Thou* —"Thou art my beloved Son"—by which he calls his Son and pours out his love upon him. It is to answer with Christ in the Holy Spirit, *"Abba, Father,"* out of the love of our hearts in every act of our conscious life.

Each time, indeed, in which man acts consciously, that is, acts as a man, he must either respond to God's presence by his own presence to God, or refuse himself to his Lord. Yet even when he tries to refuse himself to the Presence, the Presence follows him and pursues him in his flight. Thus it was early on in the case of Cain, the first of the sons of Adam who refused himself to God. No darkness indeed is able to hide man from the glory which encompasses him (Ps. 139.11).

4

THE CALL WITHIN

Even leaving aside the instances in which man wilfully refuses an answer of love to the love of the Father coming to him through events and through his encounters with his brother-men, there remain in the life of each one of us too many moments in which we are forgetful, and in which we act without actual and conscious reference to the fact that we are rational beings and indeed the children of God.

Such a habit of faith, as described above, does not develop overnight in any man. Indeed, only in time are we able to develop the possibilities of our nature and to express more and more in our minds and in our whole behaviour the deep and fundamental fact that we are children of God. Faith is no doubt in us from the day of our baptism, or from the day in which for the first time in our lives we have said to God, "Even so, Father", accepting the revelation he has made to us of his will through creation and events, and, above all, through his coming to us in the form of Jesus our Saviour. Yet the development of that faith and the full penetration by faith of all our senses and faculties can happen only in time. Such an achievement is and must be both the work of grace and the result of our efforts.

The problem, therefore, which confronts us is this: How can we develop this habit of faith which will make it possible for us to respond in every moment to the love and the presence of our Father? We possess the mind, the sense of Christ, as St Paul proclaims so boldly in the name of each Christian (1 Cor. 2.16). How then are we to develop this sense of Christ, so that we may simply, in every moment, be Christ himself looking at the Father and performing his work (John 10.37, 38)?

Sometimes God makes us aware of himself by interfering

abruptly in our lives. He has indeed his own way of awakening those who are slumbering—at least when he loves them too much to allow them to go on any longer forgetting both him and themselves. Many in fact have experienced such a call which, by cutting man off from everything on which he has so far relied, makes him stand in front of God, alone, stripped and naked. This was God's way with Paul, Augustine, Francis of Assisi, and many others. In one moment he plunged them into the reality of his Presence from which they were trying to escape, and marked their lives with an indelible seal.

Whether or not there are in our lives any such significant interventions of God, it remains for us to make every possible effort to develop our faith and our sense of the presence of God. Yet this is not to be done out of duty, nor out of obedience to the dictates of a binding law; it has rather to flow spontaneously from our love and from the deepest aspirations of our souls and hearts.

The development of this sense of faith is closely related to the care that is taken to concentrate attention on the Presence in itself. Indeed, since man is so constituted that without special discipline his efforts in any sphere are rarely fruitful, it is highly beneficial to set aside certain times, certain days or hours of the day, when he may be free from all other occupations, including vocal prayer and common worship. At such times he may devote himself with whole and undivided attention to the Presence, contented simply *to be,* his eyes turned inwards, his ears attuned to the inner silence, aware only that *God is.*

Such times cannot of course be said to be absolutely necessary in themselves. The greatest *jnanis*[1] of India, for instance, find no reason to devote part of the daily routine to this kind of exercise or *sadhana.* There are even some, like Sri Ramana Maharishi,[2] who are quite sceptical about the usefulness of such methods.

For them, in fact, nothing exists, apart from the Presence. Therefore, to set aside a few moments or hours for an exercise designed to make oneself aware of the Presence seems to them rather odd, if not meaningless. Yet it happens to them also that they are at times so overwhelmed by the Presence *in itself* that they are no longer able to pay any attention to what are only signs of this Presence, that is, to things and perceptions, sensual, or mental. The light of the sun on the snow in the high mountains is so dazzling that it makes a man blind.

Anyway, whether they are forced upon man as it were from within or deliberately chosen for their own sake, the highest times of prayer are certainly those which are devoted to the contemplation of the mystery of God in itself, when all senses and faculties are silenced. There is no doubt that it is by becoming more and more aware of the divine Presence in the secret place of our hearts that we become more and more aware of that same divine Presence surrounding us on all sides.

Was it not the promise of God to the prophet Hosea (Hos. 2.6) that he would take the soul into solitude, would hedge up all the ways whereby she used to run after her "lovers"—all the desires and thoughts of this world—and bring her to the place where she would be alone with him, face to face?

Truly speaking there is no outside and no inside, no without and no within, in the mystery of God and in the divine Presence. Yet the mind is so much distracted through the senses[3] that it needs first of all to be withdrawn from external things. Hence the need of recollecting and gathering towards their centre all thoughts and all desires. Then, after we have been inwardly fully illumined by the glory of the Presence, we realize that there are no limits to that glory, no limits to that Presence. In the light of this Splendour our very *I*, however personal it may be, seems no longer to know any boundary: it encompasses, as it were, everything on earth, attains to everything in creation, even to the core of every being, even to the centre of each heart, of each soul of man, though of course without losing its own individuality. Nothing, then, is foreign or strange to it in creation, for nothing is strange or foreign to God, and in God himself we have at long last found our home, the bosom of our Father.

Is it not really in this awareness of the divine Presence in ourselves as well as in the heart of every other man that the precept of love—the most essential, if not the only, commandment of the New Covenant—receives its full sense and shines most brightly? Jesus teaches us: "You shall love the Lord your God . . . ." and "You shall love your neighbour as yourself" (Matt. 22.37-9); he goes on to say that the second commandment is similar to the first, for it is in loving our brothers that we love God (1 John 3.17—4.20).

Each one is responsible before God for all his brothers, spiritually and temporally. He can be indifferent to none of them. They are his own flesh (Gen. 37.27); in a true sense, as explained above, they can even be said to be his own soul. This love and responsibility will be exercised, of course, at different levels, according to the closeness or distance of men to each other. Yet can it not be truly said that the man I actually meet is for me the representative of the whole of mankind? and that while loving and serving him, it is really all my brother-men whom I am loving and serving? In fact my potential neighbour is every man; anybody in the world may one day become actually my neighbour and ask from me in the name of God my personal love and service. Surely that is what the Lord taught us in the parable of the Good Samaritan (Luke 10.29)?

Those who will most truly succeed in loving their neighbours as themselves are those who have realized through their experience of the Presence within that all men are one, as the Holy Spirit himself is one, and that therefore no other man can be a stranger to them. So also only those can understand that the love of God and the love of man are one single love who in the same experience have realized that there is only *one* son of God.

Jesus is "the man for others", as we are often reminded today. But in the first place Jesus is *the man for God*. He is effectually the man for others because in the depth of his heart he has realized that God alone is and that he himself is his only Son. There is no within or without, properly speaking, in that experience of the divine Presence, which Jesus came to the world to make known to us and to share with us. As with Jesus, so with us, the hearing of God's unique Word makes us to *be* and to realize that God is everywhere and in all things, that finally he alone is.

According to the Scriptures, Christ's return to glory will bring about the summing up of all things in God. The evolution of the universe, including the whole history of mankind, is moving towards that final consummation. This is true also of each individual man in his own unique development. Each man is a microcosm and sums up in himself the whole world. The world is reaching its fulfilment whenever any conscious being passes into God. For the Christian the Eucharist is the clearest sign that the fulfilment is already present. "The hour is coming", said Jesus, "and now is" (John 5.25). In every moment of his life, in every act performed with due awareness, man is reaching his goal—which is God alone; and with him and in him the whole world is reaching it also. As soon as he hears the voice of the Son of man (John 5.25), and in it also the voice of the Father who calls him from his eternity, then man with Christ, beyond time and history, is born again, rises from the dead, and together with his Lord reaches the very place from which he originally comes, the infinite glory of God.

There is no man who has not been called to live there, in the glory, at every moment of his earthly life. Indeed some men and women are so fascinated by this Presence that they are unable to remove their gaze from it, and are therefore constrained to live their life away from normal human society. This is a sign at once of man's grandeur and of his weakness: grandeur in his origin and vocation, weakness in the inability of his spirit to bear the blinding light. Societies which, like India, the Buddhist countries, and later on the Christian world itself, have accepted and encouraged such acosmic vocations, show by that very fact the depth of their spiritual insight.

Yet it is not only monks or cloistered nuns who are called to live face to face with this Presence. All the baptized, indeed every child of God who lives on earth, has his dwelling in the bosom of that glory (cp. Col. 3.3). Each and every one is called to withdraw to the secret place of his heart, when the Spirit does not bid him perform some task in the service of God's creation. And is there anyone so constantly occupied with important duties outside that he has no time to spare for this withdrawal?

I ask for a moment's indulgence to sit by thy side.
The works that I have in hand I will finish afterwards,
as said Tagore (*Gitanjali, 5*).

Such times of inner recollection are the most truly effective
moments of our life. It is towards them that everything else in
human life is directed, but they themselves have no ulterior
object. It is the greatest mistake to suppose that moments devoted to silent prayer are merely a preparation for our work.
Meditation, for instance, is not intended to make us capable of
worthily fulfilling our duties of study, work, or social intercourse,
nor even to assist our progress in humility or any other virtue.
Contemplation is worth while in itself. It needs no further justifi-
cation. No doubt such high times of prayer will cast their rays
on the whole of life, but this radiation will not be deliberately
intended. It will happen quite spontaneously, as naturally as the
diffusion of the rays of the sun, which spread light, warmth, and
life over the whole surface of the earth.

On the other hand, the contemplation of the *Presence without* is by no means to be considered as inferior to the contemplation of the *Presence within*. Both are simply aspects of one unique
reality. Vocations differ among men. The temperament and char-
acter granted to each one by the Creator underlie his particular
vocation. Some, by natural inclination and grace, are called to
a more active way of life, and so to the contemplation and the
experience of the divine mystery in its manifestation among men.
Others are called to a more secluded life. Their contemplation
of the divine mystery will be centred more expressly on the
Presence of God to himself in himself than on the manifestation
of this Presence in the world of men. No one has any right to
despise others or to deem himself superior to or more privileged
than anyone else. In every active life there is a place also for the
pure contemplation of God in his own glory; and in every solitary life there is a place for a song to God in the glory of his
creation—"the Hymn of the Universe"—and for some participation at least in the work of men co-operating with God in the
fulfilment of his creation. There is no hermit, however far away
he may live in the depths of the forest or on the heights of the

mountain, who can forget his brother-men; even his necessary attention to the elementary needs of his body must always remind him that he is a part of creation, of the manifestation of the glory and of the love of the Lord.

These two attitudes of men are complementary and not contradictory to each other. That is true, not only of the Church or of mankind at large, but also of the individual man. At one time a man will feel like withdrawing himself from everything outside and dwelling, forgetful of everything, in the "unmanifested" mystery of God. At another he will feel drawn towards things and men, that is, towards the mystery of God's manifestation. There will be in him a kind of ebb and flow, in accordance with the condition of his mind, which will help him to keep healthy in his spiritual life, avoiding the pitfalls either of too much withdrawal, on the one hand, or of too much involvement. The truly spiritual man will feel equally at ease in either of these states. Indeed, a soul constantly aware of the presence of God in creatures will easily recollect herself deep inside, beyond any word and beyond any thought. And a soul who, passing beyond herself into the very centre of herself, has really found God in himself, will quite spontaneously discover and realize the divine Presence in all creatures and in the core of every being.

The children of God are utterly free. When the time has come for them to practise "meditation", they do it with God's joy in their hearts. But when the hour is over, or even before, if it is shortened by some necessary call, they return to their work in the world of "sign" and "manifestation" with the same joy filling their hearts. They are ever on the watch, at the disposal of the Spirit, ready to remain for ever in silence and forgetful of all things, if God so wills, but equally ready to go and serve men.

5

GOD'S REST

According to Scripture God created the world in six days and on the seventh entered into his "rest". Man is called to share both in God's activity and in his rest.

God's entering into his rest did not mean, however, that the work of creation was completely finished. The creation will be completed only when this earth and heaven have given place to the new and final earth and heaven foretold in St John's Revelation (21.1). From the Garden of Eden onwards man is called to be a co-operator with God in completing creation. God committed to Adam the care of the Garden. From him he made woman, and to both of them he entrusted the work of peopling the earth. It is only in fellowship that man is able to procreate and educate children; it is only by "corporate work" that he can cultivate the earth and can draw from its natural resources what he needs for bodily life, or for the development of his own mind. That too is a sign that man is not a *monad*, an isolated individual, but that his life is a fellowship of love modelled on the Communion of the divine Persons themselves.

But man is not only *homo faber*, a *workman*. He is not destined to be simply a labourer engrossed in his daily material work. Man is not even only a *thinker*. His destiny is not only to gather knowledge, to become a more and more powerful computer, to be a technician, or even to contemplate the "essences" or intellectual realities, according to the ideal of Plato or Aristotle. First and above all, man is the image of God, the splendour of his glory (cp. Heb. 1.1). Like him, he *is*, he is aware that he is, and in this very awakening to himself, capable of eternal bliss.

On earth, as in heaven, man is called to enter into God's final sabbath of rest and to share in his infinite stillness and bliss.

27

3

The promise, therefore, still holds good, that we are to attain God's rest . . . God's people have a sabbath of rest in store for them; to attain his rest means resting from human labours as God did from divine. We must strive eagerly, then, to attain that rest" (Heb. 4.1, 9-11; tr. by *Ronald Knox*).

No doubt men have to build together the city of man, the substructure, so to speak, of the city of God. But man can never forget that this city of God which is to be his true home is already present, even now, as St John says of the Resurrection (cp. 5.25), since the kingdom is already in the midst of us (Luke 17.21).

Since God has already entered into his rest (Heb. 4.4), every aspect of man's labour should also manifest the divine rest. The mystery of that sabbath envelops and penetrates the life of man exactly as does the mystery of the coming Kingdom. To live in the Kingdom is precisely to live by faith and in the Spirit, to live as "sons of the Resurrection" (Luke 20.30), the life which will be ours in eternity—and that is the sabbath of God. Above all, it is to live the life of God himself—of whose nature we are partakers (2 Pet. 1.4)—in the deepest recesses of our hearts, beyond thoughts, beyond words, beyond every possible manifestation of God. If God is present in the tiniest portion of what manifests him, he is at the same time beyond anything in which he manifests his presence, beyond the whole universe and beyond every part of it, beyond everything mental and beyond everything material. Everything through which God reveals himself to man is a summons to go further, to go beyond, always beyond. It is urging him to advance up the stream of God's Self-manifestation, to aim at the Source itself from which everything comes, to seek that spring which is nevertheless for ever far beyond and more ultimate than any water welling up from it.

Man is made not merely to work with his hands and to think with his mind, but also to *adore* in the deep silence of his heart. Even more than to adore he is called to plunge into that silence and to lose himself there, unable to utter any word, not even a word of adoration or of praise; for no word can express the mystery of God, the mystery of man in the presence of God, the

28

mystery of the Son in the eternal presence of the Father. There the mind cannot even think or conceive a thought, for it is over-whelmed, silenced, blinded by this light—a sun which does not allow any other luminary to be seen in the sky when it stands at its zenith.

God's work of creation and his eternal rest are complementary aspects of his one divine mystery, and it is in no way different with man. It is through building the city of men shoulder to shoulder with his brothers and also through withdrawing into the silence of the heart—both things complementary and necessary —that man has to live out his calling as the child of God, the mystery of his divine sonship.

The mystery within one man's heart—as has already been said —is the mystery within every man's heart. No man is apart from others in the place in which God abides. In the very centre of his heart, along with God, dwell also all his brother-men and the whole creation; there all times are present; what has been, what is now, what is to be, even the very consummation and fulfilment of the universe is there. The man who has made his abode in this centre of himself is by that very fact established, at the very source and origin of God's self-manifestation.[1]

Anything man does in that place shares in the power of the Spirit of God, or rather is one with it. In the centre of his soul that man has become one with the Spirit who dwells within (1 Cor. 6.16). This Spirit pervades everything on earth and in heaven. He reaches everywhere and disposes of all things at his pleasure. He is the origin of all that moves in the universe. All growth and development receives its impulse from him. Yet he himself is Silence and eternal Quiet. Therefore when a man is established in the centre of his heart, his activity may have no visible connection with the working of mind or body, and yet nothing may be more powerful and efficacious. His silent con-templation is more effective in building for all men and in the hearts of all men the city which will never pass away, than any work in the world aimed at building the human foundations of the Kingdom or even any outward preaching of the Kingdom. Whereas men commonly work through their bodies and minds, even in things related to the Kingdom, the contemplative works through the Spirit, in that very power of God which is so often mentioned in the Gospel and the Epistles. In the Spirit he overpasses time and space, he is present to all; with the Spirit he reaches from one extremity of the universe to the other (Wisdom 1.7). That is the state of the sons of the Resurrection. For that which is the mark of the time to come also characterizes in this life those who have heard the voice of the Son of Man (John 10.27) and have decided to follow him—even to the bosom of the Father where he abides in the unity of the Holy Spirit.

When man lives and abides in God's rest, he is already engaged, as it were, in what is to be his occupation for eternity. In it he has a foretaste of the life beyond, which is also the life deep within, the very life of the Father and the Son in the love and unity of the Holy Spirit. But we should never forget that such a foretaste lies far beyond the reach of our intellect or of our so-called psychological awareness. This truly is that peace of God which, as the Scriptures say, "passes all understanding" (Phil. 4.7).

It would be wrong to consider that such graces are reserved for a chosen few. They are the birthright of all Christians, indeed of all men, because it is precisely for that purpose that man has been created and to that very goal that man has been called by the infinite love of God.

In fact such graces are conferred on not a few of those who never heard of Christ's revelation;[2] it is surely impossible for Christians to deny it, though at times they are filled with wonder as to how it can have happened—just as the companions of Peter already could not understand how the Spirit had fallen on Cornelius who was not circumcised nor even baptized (Acts 10.45), and Paul himself remained his whole life amazed at the Christian vocation of the Gentiles. Yet if this is true, is it not for them an even more pressing reason to believe that every one of Christ's believers is most surely called there too?[3] Otherwise how could we justify the missions which work to extend the Church among people to whom the Spirit has already revealed such mystical treasures? Surely it is not to teach them the mere observance of certain rites and the repetition of some credal formulas. It is therefore an urgent duty for the Church and for her pastors

30

to help first every baptized man to reach the place *within* where God is waiting for him and, then, to call men to the Church from that very innermost sanctuary.

Moments consecrated by man to this special and silent prayer are indeed an offering to God, a tithe set aside from man's ordinary occupations; in them he recognizes the absolute dominion of God over everything man is or has or does, and acknowledges the essential relativity of everything which belongs to the sphere of creation or, one might say, of the manifestation of God. These times are the highest forms of "sacrifice", in which man does not offer to God material things only, renouncing their possession or enjoyment, but immolates, as it were, to him his mental possessions, even the incomparable joy of *thinking* of him. As the Scriptures say (Ps. 40.6-8), it is not man's external possessions that God asks from him in the highest act of worship, but himself, his highest self.

Contemplation is indeed the highest worship. It is in contemplative souls that the Eucharist bears fruit most fully, for in contemplation man has at last passed into the domain of God, into the Holy of Holies. Immersed in God he is no longer capable of any turning back on himself. He is not even able to say, think, or feel that he is looking at God, or that he has given himself fully to him. He is so totally aware of the divine Presence that he can now hardly even identify his own self in the dazzling light of this Presence.

Every man has some periods of leisure, but all too often he uses them unworthily. Has he never time to sit or to kneel in the presence of God's majesty—not so much to ask or to thank, but simply to remain silent before him?

Now what is true of the individual man equally applies to society at large. Some men have to be a "tithe" taken out of society, dedicated, not to preach the word of God or to build on earth the social aspect of the Church, but simply to sit silent in the Presence. In the case of such a man, it means of course an individual call and a particular vocation. Nevertheless it is in the name of their brothers that men are called to solitude and the

31

desert. It is in the name of their brothers that they plunge into the mystery of God and lose themselves in his glory.

Between the life of a Christian in the world who seeks to be led by the Spirit in the performance of his normal activities and responsibilities, and the life of the hermit, alone in his desert, in constant remembrance of God and unflinchingly attending to the inner Presence, there is an almost infinite variety of callings. The Church has in fact institutionalized a certain number of them by founding or giving recognition to the different religious orders or congregations.

Thus, on the one hand, there are friars and nuns, dedicated to the education of children, the care of the disabled, or the social uplift of the masses. At the opposite extreme there are the enclosed orders. In between come a multitude of what are called "mixed" orders. However, in the older tradition, seclusion from the world was not sufficient to earn the name of "contemplative life", or *theoria*, as it was called by the monks of the Eastern Church. Many cloistered monks and nuns in fact are just as busy behind their walls with manual and intellectual occupations as any people in the world. Their life is undoubtedly very worthy and laudable, but it always comes short of the ideal of pure contemplation. Nevertheless even in the institutes dedicated to pure contemplation a certain amount of mental and bodily activities have necessarily to be provided for; the essential thing is that such activities should always contribute directly or indirectly to an unflinching attention to the Inner Presence.

In India the highest ideal of pure contemplation has been practised and cherished by the age-long institution of *sannyasa*.[4] In the West it has been chiefly represented by the hermits of the first Christian centuries, in Syria and Egypt. Later on, although the solitary life was never totally abandoned by Christians, there is no doubt that, as the centuries passed, less and less attention was paid to this type of vocation, until finally the Roman Code of Canon Law of 1918 excluded it from the scope of "religious life" altogether, by defining the latter as a life in community.[5] It is indeed a sign of the times and a token of the divine mercy that of recent years not a few people have once again

32

heard the call to solitude; indeed lack of interest in the Church for this ideal would be a symptom of that "chilling of love" referred to in the Gospels as a sign of "abounding wickedness" (Matt. 24.12).

Among the semi-eremitical orders recognized by the Church two are specially worthy of mention. The first is the Carthusian Order, marked though it still is by the medieval emphasis on worship.[6] The other is the Carmelite Order, whose primitive rule upheld the ideal of almost unbroken solitude and contemplation; and to this day the nuns of this Order regard their cells and the prayer of silence as their most precious inheritance.[7]

It is to be hoped that the Church of India will in the end bring to the universal Church an authentically Christian *sannyasa* as the crowning of the monastic life, Thus the Church will recover after centuries the purest traditions of the Desert and of the Hesychast movement,[8] and at the same time drink deep at the inexhaustible sources of the Hindu ideal of renunciation in a life devoted to God alone. The Church is in the Spirit awaiting that ultimate inwardness of her life, in which she will discover the true depth of her own mystery, or rather will plunge into the still unsuspected depths of her own heart and of the heart of Christ. In our day more than ever before the Church needs to hear the testimony that God is beyond all things, beyond all attempts to define him in thought or word or to reach him by activity. The Church has need of an inner silence that her word may be significant, of a suspension of activity that her work may be fruitful, and of that which is beyond-all-sign so that she may reach the fulness of the sacramental sign which she herself is.[9]

Christian *sannyasa* will not, however, be an *order* in the canonical sense of the word, since its essence cannot be codified in any law or standardized in any institution. It is first of all a spirit whose manifestation and unforeseen appearance present a permanent challenge to human wisdom. Yet, at the same time, like the *prana* or vivifying *"breath"* of the Upanishads, it spreads everywhere and penetrates everything with its life, free of all constraint, yet transforming and renewing all that it touches, as much as the man in whom it reveals itself as the group among which it is manifested. It is like that "living water" to which the

33

Saviour delighted to refer, welling up in the depths of the heart, like that mystic river of water which is to gush forth at the time appointed by God from beneath the very threshold of the sanctuary—as the prophet Ezekiel foresaw in his final vision (ch. 47)—and from there to spread abroad, bringing life and healing to the whole land of promise.

6

THE OUTER COURTS

Among the forms of mental prayer which are rather widely practised in the Western Churches we must first mention *meditation,* as it is generally called—not forgetting, however, that in the common usage of India that term stands for *dhyana* and refers to the purest and highest form of contemplation.

Anyhow, as generally understood by Christians, this way of prayer consists in "meditating" or speculating on God, his existence, his attributes, his love, in trying to impress on oneself the examples of Christ and his saints, or in considering in our minds what should be our answer to the call of God, and so on.

However laudable and useful such an exercise may be, it is rather a preparation for prayer than prayer itself in the true sense. One can hardly say that it aims at making the soul aware of the presence of the living God. It tends too often to remain on the intellectual plane. It seeks to establish in the mind some strong practical convictions, capable of influencing the whole working of the intellect and will. It is more an exercise about God than a direct contemplation of God. Its efficacy is, however, beyond question. Many of those who work most for the Church have been trained and "formed" by this kind of meditation. Besides, it often provides an excellent start in the ascetic life, and it is, perhaps, the best thing at the disposal of people who are too exclusively intellectually minded. Yet we cannot but be afraid that it falls short of the real vocation of Christians, at least if it stops short and does not develop and pass into a more genuine kind of contemplative prayer. The aim of prayer, indeed, is not to think about God, not to form conceptions of God, however strong and lofty they may be. It is for God himself, for God beyond any sign and any veil, that the soul, fed by the gospel and the Spirit, is thirsty. It is God in himself whom the soul wants, the living God revealed to the Patriarchs and the Prophets, the hidden God within, the God who is realized in the contemplation of saints and sages.[1]

Meditation at times develops into a kind of affective prayer which, while deeper than the previous kind, still often remains far from the real goal. This kind of prayer consists first in interspersing the speculations and mental discourses with fervent aspirations, calls of the heart to God, acts of surrender, so-called "dialogues" with the Indweller of the soul. After some time speculations and the work of the intellect take less and less place and the prayer tends to become a simple outpouring of the heart, sometimes wonderfully sweet, sometimes agonizing, with the Lord imagined as present either within or near at hand.

Here again we have an excellent and useful exercise, provided it does not turn to sentimentalism or verbiage. It can never be recommended enough, so long, at least, as the soul has not discovered the path higher up the holy mountain. It is very useful too when owing to circumstances the mind has difficulty in concentrating and freeing itself from the images and representations which encumber it. Yet one should never forget that too often in this kind of prayer it is only an imaginary picture of God with which the soul is conversing, for example, the sweet and beautiful child in the arms of his Mother, the Saviour who suffered and died centuries ago, etc. Now it is not the Jesus who lived centuries ago who has to be the main object of my prayer, in however lively and vivid a fashion I may imagine him! It is Jesus living here and now at my side and within me that I desire, it is the God whose eternity is present in the very moment of my prayer, with whom I want to be in contact. In fact I am always in the most intimate contact with him, but I need to become aware of this contact and intimacy.

Such prayers are still like the outer courts of the Temple: the court of the Gentiles, the court of the laity. It is into the court of priests, into the Holy Place, into the Holy of Holies, that we are invited to penetrate. Christ by his cross has broken down all barriers (cp. Eph. 2.14). He has even rent asunder the veil which hid the innermost part of the sanctuary (Matt. 27.51).

No one can be satisfied till he enters the Holy of Holies. No real lover is satisfied with simply hearing of his beloved, or with simply thinking of him; he wants to take hold of him, to look at him face to face, to embrace him. "Let him kiss me with the kisses of his mouth", says the Beloved in the Song of Solomon (1.2) in the name of all the lovers of God.

Next to the prayer of the affections, of devotional aspirations, comes the prayer of petition. We are not here thinking of the recitation of formulas supposed to obtain from God as if by magic anything that we may desire. We refer rather to the out-pouring of the soul confiding all her needs to the Lord, the simple expression of everything he longs for by the child pressed to his Father's heart.

Such prayer is certainly excellent. Proud and irresponsible indeed is the man who dares to condemn or depreciate it. Did not Jesus frequently recommend his disciples to ask the Father for everything of which they were in need? On the very night before he "departed out of this world unto the Father", he reminded them again: "ask and you will receive, that your joy may be full" (John 16.24). The prayer of petition is essentially the acknowledgement of our weakness and nothingness, the realization that we come from God alone, that we depend for all on him, that he alone is our strength, and that without him we can do nothing at all, not even proclaim that Jesus is the Lord (1 Cor. 12.3). Such an attitude of soul is indeed precious before God, and cannot but be highly encouraged, chiefly when such prayer aims at the fulfilment of our spiritual needs, of the needs also of our neighbour, of the Church, of the world at large. Nevertheless is it not true that such prayer is sometimes terribly mixed with self-centredness, that the man who prays in this way may be more interested in his petty needs—the petty needs of a Christian materially and spiritually *bourgeois*—than with the adoration of the Lord? Adoration may be so much diluted with the temporal or selfish spiritual concern of the praying man that it becomes unrecognizable. To bring before God our needs and the needs of those who are dear to us may be, of course, a use-ful starting point in the path of prayer. But to save such a prayer

37

from turning into and remaining an endless self-centred conversation with oneself, it has to be purified and progressively drawn higher and higher. The prayer of petition should become, at least with time, not so much a way of "informing" God of what he knows better than we do, as an act of loving adoration of his supreme Majesty, a true act of supernatural hope and of complete surrender.

7

SILENCE AND YOGA

The spiritual tradition of the East, and especially of India, has been so strongly drawn towards the prayer of silence that it has continually striven to find methods, either physiological or psychological, which can help man to enter upon and travel safely on the way of silence. These methods are generally termed *yoga*[1] —though the word in itself is variously interpreted and is also broadly used to designate any spiritual path (for instance, *bhakti-yoga, mantra-yoga,* etc.).

As traditionally understood, *yoga* is a discipline whose essential aim is to bring the mind to complete quiet and silence. The first *sutra* of Patanjali's classical treatise on the matter put this in the most unequivocal terms: "*Yoga* is the arresting of all mental activity". However, as *yoga* is a psycho-physiological discipline, it is also responsible for some remarkable side-effects. It is certainly an unequalled method of self-mastery, whereby the will is strengthened. On the physical level also it can be a valuable aid in the harmonious development of the body; it can even restore health, and it effectively brings under control and gives suppleness to limbs and muscles. Apart from this, the most sensational yogic feats, though secondary as regards the real goal of *yoga,* are by no means mere quackery. It is these side-results which probably account in large part for the present vogue of *yoga* in Western countries. But one hopes that the initial practice of *yoga* will arouse in its adepts the desire to experience the true essence of *yoga* and will lead them by way of interior silence to the discovery of the innermost centre of the soul, which is the goal of its authentic practice.

Undoubtedly real *yoga* aims at nothing short of emptying the mind. This void is not actually wanted for its own sake, but it is firmly believed—following the experience of the masters—that, once the mind is emptied and the mental processes stopped, the deep power or light which normally lies hidden and inactive within every man rises up and shines forth by itself. Then, when this power is awakened and is able to develop freely, it brings the human being to his full perfection, or rather it makes him attain at long last to what is called his original or innate state —something like the "return to Eden" in the old Greek ascetic tradition.

Christian spiritual discipline has this at least to learn from *yoga* —to strive by any effective and acceptable means for quiet and silence in the mind. Such quiet and silence alone make it possible for the Holy Spirit to work freely in the soul. It is rare indeed for a man to keep himself fully open and responsive to the Spirit, tempted as he is too often either to rush ahead or to lag behind, in his impatience to act on his own strength. On the other hand this emptying of the mind is not in the least negative; rather it is a call, an abysmal call, as it were, from the soul's nothingness to God. The real *yogi* is one who has recovered his essential freedom, above all with regard to his own inner world of thoughts and desires. Nothing in him henceforth limits his responsiveness to the Spirit. Nothing hinders the growth in him of that inner force, the same force which holds the whole universe together and guides its development, that force which the ancient sages of India called *shakti*[2] and in which Christians can hardly refuse to recognize at least some adumbration of the Holy Spirit. The wonderful powers attributed to yogis are in a sense no more remarkable than the miracles performed by the saints; as it is believed in Indian tradition, the former have simply released within themselves the same energy which permeates the whole cosmos; whereas the latter may be said to have recovered (as it were) the state of man before the Fall, when Adam coming forth from the hands of God was sovereignly free and the master of the whole creation (Gen. 1.26).

It is quite possible to question the cosmological and psychological substructure of the theories about *yoga*, or to challenge the interweaving of the psychological with the spiritual. But no one can deny that common yogic exercises can be helpful in achieving silence in prayer. This does not mean that *yoga* is essential or that it is to be recommended to all indiscriminately. It depends on the temperament and the calling of the individual, as the best spiritual masters of India often repeat. All that matters is to reach the goal, and the practice of *yoga* must never lose sight of it.

It is every man's duty, according to his means and vocation, to keep his body healthy and to develop the capacity of his mind. It is surely no less a duty binding on every one of us to make himself capable of the awakening of his soul deep within, since that is precisely the ultimate goal assigned by God to men. Even apart from any special grace, this *experience of the self*, as we say in India, is the highest possible attainment of human beings. It is actually in that pure awareness of oneself free from all conditioning that man comes to know in experience what he actually is in himself.[3]

In any man endowed with sanctifying grace this experience of self will be taken up by the Holy Spirit to be transformed and deepened, as is the case with all man's activities. This transformation of man's faculties is what theologians call, after Isaiah 11.2, *the gifts of the Holy Spirit*.[4] Through these gifts the Spirit raises man to the capacity of living his life effectively as a child of God and a sharer in the Resurrection. He makes his intelligence able to read aright the message of the Lord which is contained in Revelation and was already foreshadowed in the creation. He gives him the necessary prudence and energy to deal in a Christian way with all situations arising in his life. Surely therefore man is obliged to train his faculties in preparation for this work of the Spirit?

The highest gift of the Spirit is the *gift of wisdom*, through which the Spirit works in the most intimate place of the soul, in that central point, where the soul is a pure awareness of itself, a pure waking up to itself, beyond all mental activities and perception. The gift of wisdom makes us experience the fact that by grace we are partakers of the divine nature (2 Pet. 1.4), the fact of our "connaturality" with God, to borrow the word of Aquinas. We may perhaps compare it to the experience of the child in the womb of its mother, fed by her directly without any activity on its side, and unable to perceive itself apart from her. Are we not then in duty bound to prepare ourselves to receive this grace, to develop the capacity of our minds for stillness, to put ourselves in a state of silent vigil, of pure waiting at the disposal of the Spirit?

For its part the aim of *yoga* is to quiet the mind, to free it from its instability and its innate tendency to dispersion, to gather it, as it were, at its very centre, to lead it, beyond all its activities, to the stillness of pure self-awareness. Opinions may differ of course about the value of particular methods of *yoga,* and it is true that many of them fall short of the goal owing to their exaggerated emphasis on some particular point, psychological or physiological. Yet the aim is unquestionable. It is simply the preparation of man for the ultimate encounter with himself, as explained by Vedanta,[5] and for the ultimate encounter with the Father in the oneness of the Holy Spirit, as Christian mystics indubitably know.

Naturally this path is not without its own risks. Nobody should ever engage in it without the help of a sure guide—the *guru*— that is, somebody who himself has trodden the path, has been granted at least a glimpse of the goal and is prudent enough to lead others. But this at least can be asserted for all devout souls, that, as long as they continue to think or feel in prayer, they are still outside the Spiritual Castle. They should never be satisfied by any wonderful thought or any marvellous sense of peace or bliss they may experience. God is beyond. As it is written in the Book of Proverbs (30.15, 16), there are three things—and a fourth one too—which never say, Enough! For even more than Sheol, the barren womb, the thirsty earth and fire, it is the soul who always says: Not yet enough; Not this, not that—*"neti, neti"*,[6] in Upanishadic language—on her way to God. Nothing can satisfy her but God himself. Yet she is for ever unable to reach him as long as she has not been willing to pass beyond herself and to plunge, lost to herself, right into the abyss of God. Then she understands, with the old patristic tradition, that silence is the highest and truest praise to the Lord, *silentium tibi laus.*

Once that is understood, the spiritual man is anxious to interweave his whole life of prayer with moments of silence; silence during his work and his routine occupations of the day; silence above all during his meditation, whatever form it may take. His silence will first be silence of the tongue, then silence of useless thoughts and desires, and finally, silence of any thought, even of the highest. This last and highest silence is the one which has to be sought as often as possible during times assigned to special meditation or contemplation. This silence will be a simple listening to the Spirit within and without, a simple looking at the One who is present within and without, simply being attentive, being aware, being awake . . . .

Some readers of course would have preferred to be given detailed and effective techniques for entering into such silence, at least for settling their minds and directing their thoughts and desires towards God alone. Yet, to speak the truth, there are no techniques in spiritual life, except perhaps for the outer layers of it. There are plenty of printed maps and guides for the antechambers of the Castle, for the external courtyards of the Temple. There are signboards on the gates outside. But once you have entered the only Guide is the Spirit. Those who have already entered may invite you—echoing the Spirit's call: "The Spirit and the Bride say 'Come' " (Rev. 22.17). But the last stages of the path, reaching to the inner shrine, is to be trodden by each one alone. In fact doors will open themselves, one after another, from inside, once faith and love are strong enough. This was expressed most beautifully by St John of the Cross:

> O happy night and blest!
> Secretly speeding, screen'd from mortal gaze,
> Unseeing, on I prest,
> Lit by no earthly rays,
> Nay, only by heart's inmost fire ablaze.
>
> 'Twas that light guided me,
> More surely than the noonday's brightest glare,
> To the place where none would be
> Save one that waited there—
> Well knew I whom or ere I forth did fare.[7]

4

Finally, there is only one way and only one means: faith—faith united with hope and love. Faith takes seriously the promises of God and the almost incredible revelation that we have been raised to the dignity of being children of God, that we have indeed been created just for that end. Hope expects nothing from any human means or agency, however powerful and sophisticated they may appear, but looks for everything to the One who calls us. By realizing the emptiness of man, hope is enabled from that very emptiness to draw out the fulness of God. Love cannot endure that the lovers should remain apart from each other, but rather it impels them to realize their union within the unity of the Father and the Son in the mystery of the Holy Spirit (cp. John 17).

8

THE WORD OF GOD

Ancient monastic tradition put great stress on what it called the *lectio divina*, the devout or divine reading, that is, reading done in the presence of the Lord and in a spirit of contemplation. In such spiritual reading, as was rightly said by old masters, there are three persons engaged: the one who is reading, the one whose words are read, and the Holy Spirit who is the bond between them.

In the life of monks of old this devout reading used in fact to take the place assigned in modern asceticism to meditation. It is indeed necessary for man's mind to assimilate the Word of God, whether it is spoken to him in the words of Scripture or in the messages of seers and saints or through the visible creation, or particularly in what he hears inaudibly in the silence of his heart. Only so will he be able to integrate that Word of God with his life and to place his total being at the disposal of the Spirit. The essential purpose of the *lectio divina* is to feed the mind with spirit and truth. Every day long periods were set apart in the monasteries for reading the Scriptures and the works of the Fathers. It was through such reading as well as by the singing of the holy Office,[1] that the monks fed their minds with divine thoughts and devout aspirations and desires. Then all those things would come forth spontaneously from their hearts at the times of silent prayer, generally after the completion of the Liturgy in the Church.

Such devout reading is not, properly speaking, the same as study, though it ought to be done with the same seriousness and attention as is normally applied to study. No religious man indeed wants to develop and feed his mind simply for the mind's sake alone. As the ancient authors put it, there is no knowledge which should not pass into love. There is no knowledge which should not go beyond the mind and reach to the very source of the mind—the heart—the "heart" of course understood in its Indian meaning (which was Pascal's too) as the centre of being, the place where God abides. In devout reading man aims first at putting himself at the disposal of the Holy Spirit, to be fed and moved by him at his will.

We know by Revelation that the Scriptures have been directly inspired by God. The writings of the saints are not indeed inspired in the same way, yet they generally issue from their personal experience of the love of God and of his presence within. All words are signs. Beyond the words and their immediate signification, it is the mystery itself latent in them that we should be eager to reach. Words and ideas will of course pass into our intellect and nest there, so to speak. Yet they ought to pass beyond it; or rather, their more important role is to provoke an awakening deep within, where no picture or idea of God is any longer possible. Then only their mission of communication is at long last fulfilled. As signs they have finally to disappear in the thing they wanted to convey: here lies the true dignity of all signs.

In the case of the words uttered by living saints, there is little doubt that their words pass directly from their hearts to the hearts of their listeners, provided the minds and hearts of those listeners are sufficiently attuned to those of the saints. Beyond what is pronounced actually by the mouth and heard by the ear, there is something, over and above, which passes, without intermediary as it seems, from the innermost centre of one to the innermost centre of the other. Yet is this so surprising? Is not God really the innermost centre of all souls? In the same way, it is through the Spirit who inspired the saints and who abides in the heart of every man that the real contact takes place between the words repeated from the saints and the mind which actually perceives them. It is indeed when one is fully receptive to the Holy Spirit that devout reading—and, let us add, any kind of spiritual meditation—becomes effective and opens the soul to the contemplation of divine realities.

There is also a place in the spiritual life of any Christian for corporate devout reading. Here again, as we have said before, particular calls must be respected, and above all the call to solitude, that is, when it is authentic and does not mask a desire to escape from or reject human brotherhood and the duty of service. Nevertheless, man lives in a world of communion and continual exchange. It is therefore natural that the faithful should from time to time gather together to meditate in common upon the holy Scriptures and other books which may help them to a better understanding of God's mystery.

We do not here mean by "corporate reading" a reading simply done in common, with some one reading aloud, and perhaps making comments, while the others listen in silence. What we have in mind here is a reading in which each one present shares, in humility and simplicity, in which all are waiting on the Spirit to be enlightened. The chief example of this is the corporate reading of the Holy Bible, but the same can be done with any spiritual book. It can even be said that the riches of sacred lore outside Christianity will never be fully understood and assimilated by Christians so long as such books are not read in that way and in that spirit.[2]

At the beginning someone reads the text. Others listen or follow in their own books. A time of silence follows in which all try to empty their minds of any distracting thought or desire, in order to become as completely as possible open to the Spirit. Then comes the time of sharing, putting questions to others, or rather, to the Spirit in others, explaining with simplicity one's own reactions to the passage which has been read. Only experience can show how much such corporate reading is able to feed the soul in its depths and enrich mutual charity—provided of course there is no one in the group who chooses to show off his own knowledge and to play the teacher for the sake of his companions.

Christians do not meditate on the word of God only in private gatherings; rather they more commonly do so, when they hear that Word proclaimed publicly during divine worship in church.

We cannot doubt that common prayer and worship are for a

Christian a fundamental duty and that the times devoted to it are the worthiest in his life. Yet it is also certainly true that no Christian—even if he is a hermit unknown to all—ever makes an act of prayer which does not of necessity embrace the whole Church, even the whole world, in its adoration and supplication. No man stands apart from the rest of mankind and no Christian stands apart from the whole mystical Body of Christ. Yet when prayer is performed in a group, there is in that performance a visible sign of the mystery of the communion of saints (cp. Matt. 18.20). That is even more true when such a group at prayer is an organic churchly group joining in what is called liturgical worship, reading or singing prayers coming from the ancient ecclesiastical tradition, repeating the very words of the saints of the Old and New Covenants. There is little doubt indeed that such corporate worship contributes excellently to the spiritual awakening of the soul.

The contemporary renewal of the Church at large which has manifested itself especially since Vatican II strongly stresses the value of official corporate worship. All kinds of experiments are being made in different places, new texts are published, new orders are tried out, with or without authorization. In these crucial years when new directions are being sought it is vitally necessary that the Liturgical Movement should be grounded in a deep experience of contemplative prayer. Otherwise it is hard to see how it can escape the dangers which lie in wait for it on every side. Not a few of the current liturgical novelties appear to be rather shallow and give little sign of fostering that prayer in spirit and in truth which God requires from his children.

Traditional liturgical prayer emerged directly from the contemplation of the medieval monks. Admittedly it laid stress on themes which are no longer fashionable—for instance, man's weakness and sin; its scope also was too often limited to the horizons of "Christendom" while its forms failed to express the fulness of human, or even of Christian, togetherness or *koinonia*. This at least is true of the liturgies of the recent centuries. It is therefore wholly to be expected that new forms and formulas should seek to integrate the values which are of importance to humanity today, such as the dignity of the human person, the goodness of creation, the need for Christian concern for the world, and social justice. Yet all this has first to be assimilated interiorly in prayer, so that its liturgical expressions may not be simply the repetition of popular slogans, but may be a vehicle for truly personal prayer which springs from the contemplation of those same values as they are grounded in the mystery of God himself. The more spontaneous liturgical prayer becomes, the more must it be rooted in contemplative experience, or it will end in shallowness and verbosity. Now that all structures and formulas are being challenged, where can the Christian find the firm footing that he needs, or his true identity, except in the fundamental experience of the Presence in himself, all around him, in everything and beyond everything?

Liturgy should express above all that inner experience, and should lead men to it. New forms of prayer should stress the inner mystery and the wonder of the Presence (on which the traditional forms were all too silent!), and should help Christians to taste it and long for it, so that in their petitions they beg for a deeper knowledge of these realities rather than for deliverance from those vague spiritual and temporal dangers to which the old forms so often refer. Meditative chants after the readings, enabling the worshipper to savour the mystery, should be drawn not only from biblical sources but also from texts in the "cosmic covenant", whose authors have experienced the mystery and have expressed it in terms capable of arousing a like hunger in their brethren. Times of silence for all, which now at last have been recognized as entitled to a place in common worship, should be still further extended, especially among contemplative groups and communities. In their case the use of words could be reduced to the essential minimum. After such worship the faithful should go on their way fully recollected within themselves. Then only will the Church's liturgy recover its proper function in Christian life and the old reproach which contrasted its legalism and ritualism with the spontaneity and the depth of true prayer, be no longer heard.

Liturgical prayer has a pre-eminent place in the life of the Church, and therefore in the life of every Christian. Yet each individual has his own particular spiritual needs and divine calling. It is no doubt the duty of every Christian to take part in the worship of the Church as a community, and principally in the celebration of the Holy Eucharist which is its heart. However, it remains for each one to decide in his responsibility before God and according to his conscience—bearing in mind of course what the Church lays down as a minimum for all—what part of his prayer should be in listening to the Word of God and worshipping in company with others, and what part should be kept for silent prayer in his own room with the door shut, as the Master has taught.

In the Church certain Religious Orders exist for the offering of divine praise in corporate worship, for instance, the Canons Regular or the Benedictines.[3] Others are consecrated to silent contemplation, like the Carmelites, at least according to the original intention of the Order.

The Church is like an immense tree which provides shelter and food for all sorts of birds. The mystery of God is infinite, and so is also the mystery of the Church which is the fulness of Christ (Eph. 1.19—2.9). Its manifestations also vary infinitely, and this is surely good. Some ways of prayer—especially corporate prayer—show more clearly that the life of man is a life of communion with God and with his fellow men in God. On the other hand, silent prayer—for instance, the prayer of the hermit in his solitude—witnesses to the mystery of the divine aloneness —that of God in himself, and of man within him—beyond any sign, any thought, any word; and yet this prayer, no less than corporate prayer, is made in the name of all Christians and of all men.

9

THE PRAYER OF THE NAME

There are indeed no methods, yet there is something which can help us and lead us further and further into the sanctuary of the soul, something which can bring us to the summit of Mount Horeb (cp. 1 Kings 19.8). We refer here to an age-long tradition both of India and of the Christian East.

In India this is called the *namajapa*,[1] the prayer of the Name. It consists of repeating continuously the name of the Lord, either alone or enshrined in a formula of praise, for instance: "Rama, Rama"—"Hare Krishna"—"Namah Shivaya". Often the devotee counts his *mantras* on a sort of rosary, or else he may assign to himself some period of time in which he will repeat the name without ceasing. Some aim at achieving a given number of invocations every day. Some go on repeating endlessly the holy Name: they continue repeating it during the time they are working or walking about, whispering it even when they converse with others, interrupting it only when obliged to give an answer. As far as possible the *Name* is given by a *guru*. Then it is either an initiation into a particular name of the Lord given by the *guru* to any worthy disciple who applies to him, or it is a special *mantra*[2] conferred by the *guru* on a given man, in accordance, at least theoretically, with the disciple's needs and aspirations.

The best counterpart in Christianity of the Hindu *namajapa* is what is called in Russia and in the Near East the *Jesus Prayer*. It is the endless repetition of the holy Name of the Saviour. Here again it is either the mere utterance of the name of Jesus, or it is a more complex invocation in which the name of Jesus is inserted. The most common formula, in recent centuries, is the following: "Lord Jesus, Son of the living God, have mercy on me, a sinner".

One immediately notices the stress on sin and forgiveness found in the Christian prayer of the Name. But asking for forgiveness is not a sign of an unhealthy concern with oneself, as is sometimes asserted. It rather arises from, and leads to, the discovery that God is love, and that it is by forgiving that he manifests most fully both his love and his omnipotence.[3] In the last analysis, to pray for forgiveness is to become aware of the deepest mystery of the Godhead.

On the other hand, the Hindu, for his part, is content simply to praise the Lord: "Glory to Shiva", "Namah Shivaya!" Here the simple stress on praise and adoration has nothing to do with the confidence of the Pharisee in his own righteousness which feels no need for the divine mercy. At least in those who are really spiritual, it is rather the sign of a complete self-forgetfulness and lack of concern with oneself. Once God has been realized, who could even think of himself in the presence of the Almighty?

The Christian prayer of the Name comes from a very ancient tradition. It originated among the monks of Egypt and St John Climacus recommends it in his *Scale of Perfection*.[4] Later on it was widely practised in the monasteries of Mount Athos. It was the soul of the Hesychast movement, and among its protagonists it is sufficient to mention Simeon the New Theologian and Gregory Palamas.[5] In recent centuries it has spread more and more widely among the Orthodox Churches, especially in Russia, which is the source of that gem of a book, *The Way of a Pilgrim*.[6]

The forms of the Christian *japa* varied very much, especially in its beginnings, until it became a formula centred on the name of Jesus, as quoted above. It was perhaps the finest flower of the practice of brief ejaculatory prayers which were so warmly recommended by the Desert Fathers. Some of them spent their time crying to Heaven the *Miserere* ("Have mercy on me, O Lord"; Ps. 51.1). Some made constant use of the first verse of Psalm 70: "Be pleased, O God, to deliver me! O Lord, make haste to help me!" For others the common invocation was the *Trisagion*,[7] in either of its forms: the "Holy, holy, holy is the Lord" of the vision of Isaiah (6.3), or the "Holy is God! Holy

52

and Almighty! Holy and Immortal!" of the oriental liturgical tradition. But all these prayers were fundamentally the same: a short appeal or a short act of praise to God, which a man repeats continuously, to fix his mind on the Lord and to offer him the homage of his love.

In India, as well as in the Christian Near East, the prayer of the Name is of different kinds and degrees. To begin with, it may be uttered either by the lips, or in the mind, or in the heart. No one of these ways excludes the others; yet the "place" in which a devotee habitually whispers this prayer can normally be taken as an indication of the depth at which he is aware of the divine Presence.

The first step is to pray with the lips, to repeat the name of the Lord loudly, or at least audibly. The mind may be distracted and may move at its own pace; the heart may be full of desires, which are far from consistent with the prayer uttered by the tongue. It does not matter. The utterance of the holy Name will do its work by itself in its own time. The only important thing is that the devotee should repeat the Name with respect and a real longing for the grace of the Lord.

In the second step the lips remain closed. It is in the mind, in the head, as it were, that the prayer is whispered. The prayer has now become a thoughtful attention to the Name which is being repeated. However, it is not so much a mental consideration of the meaning of the Name as a simple awareness of it. Sometimes to help his concentration the devotee will imagine either the chosen words in written form or a picture corresponding to them.

Then there is the third stage, when the prayer, or rather the Name, is placed in the heart. There is no longer any movement of the lips or of the vocal cords, or even at its best any movement of the mind. The prayer is lodged there in the very centre of the being. Not only is the mind now completely quiet, but all desires too have been transformed and have passed into the sole desire for the Lord, the desire to contemplate his glory, to merge into it. To help place the Name in the heart, saints who have practised it recommend that it be uttered (though inaudibly) according to the rhythm of the respiration or of the beating of the heart. Thus it is the whole being—body and soul, senses and mind as well—which is taken up into the prayer, and through the body, the whole universe also, of which the body is a part.

The mystery and virtue of the prayer of the heart can be conveyed only through images, for concepts would be even more misleading. The underlying idea is evidently that we must never be contented with living, even less with praying to and meeting God, on the surface of our being, at the level merely of our senses and minds. The real place of the divine Encounter is in the very centre of our being, the place of our origin, from which all that we are is constantly welling up. Physically this is symbolized by the heart. Thus to direct the attention towards the heart, even in a physical way, is symbolically to turn all our activities towards the very centre of ourselves. This centre is really the point of which of course we can form no image, in which the soul is, as it were, coming from the hands of God and waking up to itself.

India too, from the beginning of her spiritual meditations, has been alive to the mystery of the heart, the *guha*,[8] the "cave" within, as it is called in her scriptures. That *guha* is what is beyond the reach of sense or thought. It is the "abode of *Brahman*,[9] the very place of the *atman*[10] itself, the truest self of man. It is the source of everything in the *macrocosmos*, which is the whole universe, and in the *microcosmos*, which is man himself. In it is the Life from which has issued every manifestation of life. In it is the Fire from which all things get warmth and are kindled. In it is the Light by which everything shines and becomes visible.

Indian tradition has given even more precise details about the place in which the *mantra* may or must be recited. There is the theory of *cakras* or centres through which the divine power or *shakti* is supposed to develop and to rise progressively up the body. The last centre, or *cakra*, according to tantric tradition, is situated between the two eyes at the base of the nose. Here is placed the "third eye" of Shiva, his spiritual eye, the one which opens inside and sees everything in the light of the brightness within. There is also a supreme *cakra*, but this is not counted with the others. It is situated at the very top of the cranium, just below the opening point through which the spirit (*purusha*) entered the body (*Aitareya Upanishad*, 1, 3. 12) and through which the soul is supposed to flee at the time of release. The *guru's* teaching and even more one's own personal experience alone can unveil the spiritual truth hidden behind this imagery. It is enough to have mentioned it here.

The fruits of the prayer of the Name differ according to the degree of the prayer and the "place" in which it is uttered; but at all levels they are infinitely precious. In the first place, it helps beginners to fix their wandering attention; it also leads advanced souls up to "the experience of the Holy Spirit", as the Russian mystics are accustomed to say.

If worthily practised, the repetition of God's name is certainly a wonderful help in concentrating the attention and deepening the mind. We are creatures with fickle minds and are constantly liable to distraction. To live on the spiritual plane means to resist and to fight this weakness; such is the goal of any ascetic life. We can carry on this struggle through contrary mental processes, as was mentioned above, when speaking of "meditation". But while doing so, we still remain on the level of the mind and run the risk of never "taking off".

The prayer of the Name, for its part, gives the mind just the kind of food it needs, and keeps it busy enough not to look for other outlets, without at the same time impeding the quest within. By repeating the Name, the mind becomes more and more one-pointed, *ekagra*. Distractions vanish, or, if images keep on recurring in our thoughts, they are rather like passing dreams with little effect on our actual concentration. The mind, once stabilized, plunges spontaneously within itself, towards its centre. The wording of the *mantra* will then probably convey less and less of its original meaning. That does not matter at all. From the external meaning of the word the soul is now reaching up to its essential meaning, from the form conveyed by a particular name, to the mystery beyond all forms, whose sign indeed the name is. At long last, through the grace of the Holy Spirit, the mind goes to sleep, as it were, and all memory of itself disappears. Then it attains the true prayer, of which Antony the

Great used to say: "The only real prayer is the one in which we are no longer aware that we are praying."[11]

The prayer of the Name is therefore the best way to enter into meditation, in those periods which may be devoted to that exercise. It is also the best way to remain at all times aware of the presence of God. Such prayer indeed should always be on our lips, in our minds, in our hearts, during all occupations which do not require special attention on our part. There are so many hours in the day in which it is quite immaterial in itself whether we think of one thing or another; times when we are walking or travelling, times immediately before and after sleep, times of manual occupations like gardening, sewing, cleaning, times devoted to the needs of the body, etc. We could transform into conscious prayer all those times of our lives when our minds are not fully engaged. Thus we would also avoid the many distracting thoughts which continuously enter our minds and trouble us so much at the times specially assigned to prayer. So many useless or harmful desires would then be stifled at their very conception. As soon indeed as they appear, the recollection of the Name will confront them and they will be dashed on it as on the rock which is Christ, as St Benedict explains in commenting on Psalm 137 (*Rule*, ch. 7).

Of course the prayer of the Name must not impair the application of the mind to its necessary duties. It is evident that the prayer of the Name cannot continue at such times at least on the tongue or in the thinking intellect, and it is just here that we find the marvels of the prayer of the heart. It can go on at all times even when the mind is consciously at work, or even when it is lost in sleep: "I slept, but my heart was awake . . . ." was said by the bride in the Song of Solomon (5.2). Even when the mind is not aware of it, the prayer of the heart remains as a kind of background or substratum which underlies everything. It is like the rocky bed of a river which itself never moves, but over which the waters flow without ceasing. For some people the continuous flow of the *mantra* is so intense that they "hear" it, as it were, through all their mental processes.

Psychologically, there is no doubt that the prayer of the Name possesses an incomparable value. But its value is not merely practical. If it were, it would fall short of the praises given to it by the saints, and would be unable to produce the marvellous results described above. The Name is like an icon. Icons are signs and, as such, possess something of the reality they are intended to signify and represent. Of course they can become idols, when one stops at them. Yet they are a wonderful aid granted to us by the Lord, to help our feeble and fickle intellects in their groping towards him and in their longing to get at least some glimpse of his glory.

The Name is the supreme mental icon. That is specially true when the Name has been directly revealed by God, like the name of Yahweh in the Old Covenant and the name of Jesus in the Gospel. Yet we can hardly imagine that those who have not had direct access to the riches of evangelical revelation have been completely forsaken by their Father in heaven. We cannot otherwise understand how God so often made use of the *namajapa* to bestow on Hindus, for instance, some of his most precious spiritual favours. The names of God rose in the heart of sages and *rishis* from their deep experience of the Spirit. They tried to express in them something of their inner vision. They called God "Shiva", the Benevolent One, the Auspicious One; "Rama", the Lovely One. They charged those syllables with all the spiritual power of their love and of their adoration. Others after them continued repeating those names and they also enriched them with their own faith and inner experiences. Disciples received them from their *gurus* in the sacred rites of initiation, or *diksha*. Successive generations of men were called to draw out spiritual energy from them and to make them in return more and more expressive of the highest Mystery.

The name indeed is believed to contain in itself as in a nutshell the whole divine Mystery, to carry, as it were, in a concentrated form, everything that man can say or think of that Mystery, in the same way as a pearl, small though its volume is, is worth a large quantity of gold or other precious material. For the man who has tasted the prayer of the Name, the Name will mean all that theologians try to develop in countless volumes.

But it will convey it no longer in a diluted and derived form. It will satisfy his thirst with water from the very fountain-head.

That is the reason why the *namajapa* is of itself so powerful. Of all *mantras* and prayers, the invocation of the Name is the most efficient. Psychologically it concentrates and deepens the mind. Furthermore, by the very power it enfolds within itself, it leads the soul towards the very centre, the origin, the unique Source.[12] It endows her with a spiritual energy which will never stop short of divine union. To come back now to biblical ways of speaking, is not the power of the Name the very power of the Holy Spirit present in us? It is in the Spirit alone that we are able to utter the name of Jesus.

10

OM! ABBA!

The highest *mantra* among Hindus is OM, the *pranava*. More than any particular name of the Divinity it conveys the ineffability and the depths of the divine Mystery. It bears no special distinct meaning, as do the names of Shiva and Rama mentioned earlier. It does not even recall any mythological or semi-historical event. It is a kind of inarticulate exclamation uttered when man is confronted with the Presence in himself and around himself. OM is, as it were, the simplest sound utterable by man: beginning with A, the primordial sound (cp. *Tirukkural* 1.1),[1] it deepens into O and is lengthened by a nasal resonance, the *bindu*.

The most frequent explanation of the *pranava* is that it is formed of three elements: A and U,[2] which united together give the diphthong O, then the M: three letters and a single sound. It is therefore said to symbolize all possible triads, in place and time—for instance what was, what is, and what will be—and then what is beyond all triads (cp. *Mandukya Upanishad*, 1), because God is in everything and yet is beyond everything. It is also sometimes said that OM is not composed of three parts only, but of four, the fourth one being the silence in which all utterances merge. The OM which is uttered or heard comes from and goes to the OM which is neither pronounceable nor audible.[3]

OM is then the first word pronounced by God, his *Vag*, when he begins to reveal himself in his manifestation either in creation at large or in the origin of each soul. All sounds are included in the primordial *Vag*, the brahman-sound or *shabda-brahman*, as it is also called: from it all words emerge and receive their significance. OM is what is first heard of God when he appears to man as coming out of his silence. At the other end OM is the last sound which man is able to utter when, answering the call of the Spirit, he lets himself be introduced into the silence of the Godhead. So also the Bible teaches that all things come from the "Word" of God (John 1.2): "For he commanded and they were created" (Ps. 148.5); "And God said: Let there be light, and there was light" (Gen. 1.2).

Christians have before now speculated on possible Christian interpretations of OM. Some like to see in it, in the symbol of its three elements merged into one simple sound, some shadow of the trinitarian mystery.[4] We may equally see in it the Word who eternally proceeds from the silence of the Father, as was so beautifully expressed by Ignatius of Antioch (*Letter to the Magnesians*, 8), and through whom all our adoration and prayers rise towards the Almighty. But even in the Christian view OM remains above all the symbol of our last step in the spiritual ascent. As the *Katha Upanishad* says, "It is the last support, it is the highest one" (2.17; *Prasna Upanishad* 5.7). OM stands for God the Unmanifest, the essential Beyond, to whom everyone who has had even a glimpse of the Presence is insistently called and irresistibly tends.

The *mantra* OM goes back to the most ancient Vedic times. It was—and still is—uttered at the beginning and at the end of every scriptural recitation. Uttered by the priest who led the sacrifice, OM was expected to give efficacy to all rites (*Prasna Upanishad*, 5.6). It is still the most cherished *mantra* of spiritual and ascetic men. They first use it as part of their habitual *mantras*: *OM namah Shivaya, Hari OM*, and so on. When the call to a higher life is heard by them, they will abandon all prayers, all rites, all practices of devotion, but they will keep on whispering indefinitely the sacred OM, whether walking, sitting, admiring nature, plunging their minds into deep meditation, attending to the bare needs of their bodies, or answering the greetings of the passer-by. Then when the time comes for their departure, OM is still the last sound uttered by their dying lips before they pass into the silence of the eternal Now of God.

However OM is not a *mantra* on the same level as any other *mantra* which the devotee can decide to repeat a given number of times and on a rhythm of his own choosing—for OM is unique. Indeed, if we speak of OM in the plural, it is only in the same way as Being itself is so spoken of on the level of manifestation.[5] As experience deepens, OM appears as the reflection in man's mind of the universal theophany or revelation of *Being* in the world of *becoming*, the echo in his own heart of the heart-beats of the universe. OM is the awakening of every man in the secret place of his heart, the *guha*, to the mystery that is hidden in each movement of the creation, revealing at any point of space or time its divine origin and final goal. OM is the sound which, at the ultimate boundary of meaning gives everything its truth. OM, for anyone who has awakened to God, expresses the fulness of his communion with the whole universe, and also his communion with every other man who thinks, desires, and loves. In the rhythm of man's body and soul, of his heart-beats, his breathing, and his thinking, in the rhythm also of the cosmos, of the inner vibrations of atoms and living cells as well as of the galaxies, OM calls everything that is to reach its fulness, and to do so even in the most fleeting act or moment of time. Expressed in Christian terms, could it not be said that OM is the prayer of man, and through man of the whole creation, for the coming of that final kingdom proclaimed by Jesus, for the gathering and summing up of all things in Christ, and in him the return of all to the Father, the Source and the Consummation of all (cp. 1 Cor. 15.28)?

Nevertheless the use of the *pranava* cannot be recommended indiscriminately to Christians, or of course to any others. This *mantra* is too rich and too exalted for anyone to be capable of using it unless he has at least begun to taste the inner experience to which it refers. Otherwise it remains an empty sound, having no spiritual echo in the man who utters it. But if the Christian has tasted the spiritual tradition of India, and better still, if he has accepted the full implications of the gospel's message and has allowed the Spirit to lead him into the depths of his own heart, then he is as much entitled as his Hindu brother to sing or whisper the OM, the ultimate symbol of the abysmal depth of God and the self. No doubt in times of reflection and meditation he will give to this *mantra* a fuller meaning, a meaning enriched

61

by all that revelation has taught him concerning the mystery of God; and yet, once the OM wells up, as it were, at his heart's centre, will not OM be for him also a mystery of pure silence?

It is perhaps more difficult to choose among traditional Christian *mantras* and to decide which of them is the highest and most to be recommended. Here again individual callings have to be respected, and also the ever-changing needs of the soul on her spiritual path. The symbols used in prayer ought to reflect the experience that is there at depth at any given time and should help her to progress every moment a little further in her tasting of the mystery within. Yet many will maintain that the name of Jesus is the most sacred utterance expressible by the mouth of men. It is on the basis of that belief that the so-called "Jesus Prayer" has been developed so wonderfully among Eastern Christians. Yet is not Jesus the Way to the Father? Was not Jesus' main ministry on earth to lead men to the Father, who is "greater" than he, as he says so mysteriously in St John (14.28)? Truly the name of Jesus itself reveals the Father: Jesus, *Yehoshua*, "Yahveh saves". The name of Jesus is like the summing up of everything that God wanted to manifest of himself to man. Yet, as has been so often pointed out already, however adorable is the mystery of God in what is manifested of it, God remains always beyond, beyond . . . .

Twice in his letters (Rom. 8.15; Gal. 4.5), St Paul reminds us that the Spirit is constantly whispering in the depths of our hearts the sacred invocation, *"Abba, Father"*. *"Abba, Father"* was, to be sure, the ceaseless prayer of Jesus also. It is enough indeed to glance through the Gospels to realize that the remembrance of the Father was always in the heart and mind of Jesus, and his holy Name on his lips. Alike in his times of solitary prayer, and when he was in the midst of the crowds, for example, before performing miracles (John 12.27-8), he was at all times calling on the Father. *"Abba"* was his last prayer in Gethsemane (Mark 14.36), his last word on the cross (Luke 23.46). Is not that an invitation to Christian believers to make the invocation *"Abba Father"* the centre of their spiritual lives—to make it their most cherished *mantra* ceaselessly on their lips, in their minds, in their hearts? By doing so they will follow and imitate Jesus, not only in the external aspects of his life, but in what was the very core of his whole life. By repeating with him *"Abba, Father"*, they will penetrate more and more his most intimate secrets, the secret above all of his being at the same time one with the Father and also the Father's beloved Son. Their hearts will be thus transformed into the heart of Jesus himself. In this way they will really pray in the name of Jesus; that is, *with* Jesus, *in* Jesus, they will offer to the Father the homage of their prayer and adoration. More than any other *mantra* or prayer, the *"Abba, Father"* will make them partakers of the mysterious life of the Father and the Son, face to face with each other. *"Abba, Father"* will be their constant response to the *"Thou art my beloved Son"* by which the Father addresses them, in his only Son, from all eternity. It will also be their answer to the call arising from their own hearts, which are made by God and made for God; at the last it will be their answer to the call arising from the whole creation, through all beings, through all events of life and history, through all their encounters with their brother-men, because through and in everything it is always God, the Almighty Father, who comes to them and who calls them to him.

"Abba, Father" is then the sacred *mantra* which opens the doors of eternity, the doors of the inner sanctuary, the doors of the cave of the heart, and makes the soul share in the most intimate life of God in himself—a secret hidden from all generations of man, till the Son of God in person appeared as a man amongst men.

Could we not say that OM introduces man into the mystery of the Holy Spirit, the Unspoken and Unbegotten Person, who will reveal to the elect the mystery of the Son, and whispers in the sanctuary of the heart the eternal ABBA? ABBA then is the last word uttered by the creature, for it leads directly to the unfathomable mystery of the Father.

ABBA is the mystery of the Son, OM the mystery of the Spirit. But ultimately there is no name for the Father, for the Father can never be known in himself. He is known only through his self-manifestation in the Son and in the Holy Spirit.

The Father is that last or fourth part of OM, which is pure Silence.

5*

NOTES

CHAPTER 1

1. *Darshan* (Sanskrit *darshana*): vision, sight. A term that is used when a devotee comes into the presence of God; it is also applied to holy images or places, or to holy persons.

CHAPTER 2

1. Note that the solemn prayers of the Church addressed to the Father end with this formula: "through Jesus Christ our Lord, who lives and reigns with you *in the unity of the Holy Spirit . . .*".

2. *Koinonia:* a Greek term used in the New Testament (derived from *koinos,* common). It means communion, fellowship, communication, "being/having together". It expresses the deep participation of Christians in each other's life, in Christ's life, in the Father's life, which is brought into being by grace, and which love (in the N.T., *agape)* makes actual. It is this *"koinōnia* of the Holy Spirit" which St Paul desires for the Christians of Corinth (2 Cor. 13.13) and which the same Spirit works to produce in the whole universe and especially in the souls of the elect.

3. Cp. the article "Faith, Baptism and Conversion", in the *Indian Journal of Theology* (July 1967).

4. Ignatius, bishop of Antioch in Syria, martyred at Rome about A.D. 110, who on his way to martyrdom wrote seven letters which are among the greatest treasures of the Church.

5. Bultmann, *Jesus and the Word,* iv. 1 (Fontana edn, p. 98). See the context, pp. 98-9:

> For the Greek it is . . . axiomatic that God, like other objects of the world, can be examined by the thinking observer, that there can be a theology in the exact, im-

mediate sense . . . . Judaism has from the beginning a different conception of God: He does not in any sense belong to the world of objects about which man orients himself through thought . . . . In reality Greek thought always regards God in the last analysis as a part of the world or as identical with the world, even when, or rather, especially when He is held to be the origin and formative principle which lies beyond the world of phenomena. For here too God and the world form a unity within the grasp of thought; the meaning of the world becomes clear in the idea of God.

The Hindu experience of God is in this respect quite akin to the biblical, and both are irreducible to the conceptualization or objectification of God in Greek philosophy. God is hidden in his own mystery. No one has ever seen him—except the one who is in the Father, and is eternally one with him (John 1.18). Only faith can find him in his real being, a faith based on the Scriptures which are the self-revelation of God to man. Faith becomes more and more luminous by radiating the splendour of the Spirit within. It comes to its climax in the highest experience of the Spirit within the experience of self-awareness. Until that point is reached, there is always the danger of superimposing our own conceptions upon the reality of God or of the self—the conscious personal being, which is made in the image of God. This *adhyaropa* or *adhyasa* (superimposition), as it is called in Indian philosophy, only ceases when the Light within (within the self and within all things) is seen in all its fulness and brightness. When the sun is at its zenith, one's body no longer casts any shadow on the ground. This sense of the divine Presence, always at the same time immanent and transcendent, is the determining factor in all Indian approaches to theological and spiritual problems. (Cp. "An Approach to Indian Spirituality", in *The Clergy Review* (Feb. 1969).

6.   That really which is called Brahman,
         that indeed is the space external to man;
         that indeed which is the space external to man,
         that really is the space internal to him;
         and that space which is internal to him
         is verily this space within the heart.
         That is the Full . . . (*Chandogya Upanishad*, 3.12. 7-9).

Now the light which shines beyond the heavens, on the back of all things, on the back of every single thing, in the highest worlds, than which there is no higher—that is indeed the same as the light within man (ibid., 3.13.7).

> Now in this city of Brahman
> there is a dwelling place,
> a tiny lotus flower,
> within it a tiny space:
> seek what is within it . . .
> As wide as the space outside
> is that space within the heart,
> within it lie heaven and earth,
> fire and wind, sun and moon,
> lightning and the stars,
> everything . . . . (ibid., 8.1.2-3).

The knower of Brahman attains the highest . . . . he who knows Brahman as the real (*satyam*), as knowledge (*jnana*), as the infinite (*ananta*), placed in the cavity of the heart in the highest heaven (*nihitam guhayam parame vyoman*) . . . . (*Taittiriya Upanishad*, 2.1).

7.   Thither the eye does not go,
        Speech does not go, nor the mind.
        We do not know, we do not understand,
        How one can teach this.
        Other than the knowing, verily, it is,
        And also above the unknown.
        Thus have we heard from the ancients
        Who have discriminated it for us . . .
        What can not be known by the mind,
        And whereby, they say, the mind is known,
        That alone know ye as Brahman,
        Not that which those people worship . . .
        If you think, "I know well!"
        Only little, in truth, you know of Brahman.
                (*Kena Upanishad*, 1.3, 5; 21).

8. *Pleroma:* literally, fulness (cp. Sanskrit, *purnam*). A term used in Pauline theology which refers to the Church, the mystical Body of Christ, ever growing on earth until Christ in it brings it to its fulness (Eph. 1.23; 4.13; Col. 1.24).

CHAPTER 3

1. Veronica was a pious woman who, according to tradition, came to Jesus on his way to Calvary and wiped with a cloth his holy face, stained with dirt and blood.

2. Compare the Johannine expression *facere veritatem*, "to do the truth" (John 3.21; 1 John 1.16) and the whole treatment of truth in chapter 8 of the Gospel (see also Eph. 4.15).

3. God is love, as St John explains in his First Epistle (4.16). St Paul even hints at some kind of identification between love and being, when he says "If I have no love, I am not!" (1 Cor. 13.2).

   We may be allowed here to quote one stanza of a Tamil mystic, Tirumular, who a few centuries later expressed the same truth in a remarkable way:

   > The one who says that Shiva and Love are two,
   >   Verily, knows nothing!
   > Who will indeed ever understand
   >   What is Shiva and what is Love?
   > Only he who has discovered
   >   That Shiva is Love and Love is Shiva,
   > Attains to the Peace,
   >   One for ever with Shiva-the-Love.

4. The real inspiration of the many beautiful Vedic hymns addressed to the Sun, which are still in use among Hindus, consists in the fact that under the names of Surya, Aditi, Pushan, or Savitri, they address, not the material disc of light which our eyes perceive, but the mystery of Light, of life, of mensuration, of the source and direction of the universe.

   > Looking at the transcendent Light
   >   Beyond the darkness,
   > the Light which is most excellent.
   > (*Rig-Veda*, 1.50. 10; tr. A. C. Bose in *The Call of the Vedas*).

   > Most gracious God, who brings (the world) to life and keeps (it) in repose;
   > He who controls what moves and what is still;
   > May he, Savitri, the God, grant us peace!
   >   (ibid., 4.53.6)

Savitri! God! send far away all evil!
  Send us what is good (ibid., 5.82.5)

He who sees all from above and inside,
  sees all living things together;
May he, Pushan, be our Saviour! (ibid., 3.62.9)

Him, the Supreme Ruler, the Inspirer of the intellect,
  we invoke for our aid. (ibid., 1.89.5)

With a vessel of gold
is hidden the face of Truth.
O Pushan, uncover it,
that I may behold it!
Spread out and gather thy rays,
that I behold the Light,
of thee the loveliest form! (*Isa Upanishad*, 15-16)

The summit of God's whole manifestation in creation is
Christ and it is the mystery of Christ in the end that Christians contemplate and adore within and beyond all that is per-
ceived by sense or intellect.

Christ is indeed the true Light, as he himself proclaimed
(John 8.12). The first Christians were deeply conscious of this
truth. They used to praise him in their hymns under the
symbol of Light, as in the ancient Greek evening hymn,
Phōs hilaron. They were also accustomed to assemble for
worship at sunrise and sunset, an almost universal custom
whose traces still remain today in Christian liturgies (cp. the
Hindu *sandhya*).

Christian theology is at times so overwhelmed by the dazzling light of God's revelation in history, as recorded in the
Bible, that it almost forgets the splendour of his manifestation in the Cosmos. Yet Christ is the Lord of the Cosmos;
indeed, it is only because he is this, that he is also the Lord
of History. In him and through him all things were made
(John 1.3); to him all things return, and in him all things
consist (Col. 1.7). In his image, as he is the Image of the
Father, all things have been created.

The cosmic religions, which of course are unaware of Christ
as the Lord of History, nevertheless worship him, without
knowing his revealed Name, as the Lord of the Cosmos; and
perhaps they are the intermediaries through whom the Spirit

is reminding Christians not to belittle this fundamental aspect of the mystery of Christ.

5. Compare Tagore, *Gitanjali,* 45:

> Have you not heard his silent steps?
>> He comes, comes, ever comes.
> Every moment and every age, every day and every night,
>> He comes, comes, ever comes ....
> In the fragrant days of sunny April through the forest-path,
>> He comes, comes, ever comes.
> In the rainy gloom of July nights on the thundering chariot of clouds,
>> He comes, comes, ever comes.
> In sorrow after sorrow it is his steps that press upon my heart and it is the golden touch of his feet which make my joy to shine.

CHAPTER 4

1. *Jnani* (from *jnana*, wisdom): one who is endowed with full spiritual wisdom, a "realized" soul.

2. Ramana Maharishi: a sage of Tamilnad, who lived in Arunachala (Tiruvannamalai) and passed away in 1950. See for his teaching: *The Spiritual Call of India* (1972), chapters 2 and 3.

3.
> The Creator pierced outward
>> the holes of the senses;
> Therefore man looks outside,
>> not within himself.
> Yet yearning for deathlessness
> a sage turned his look within,
> and straight beheld the Self (*Katha Upanishad,* 4.1).

CHAPTER 5

1. We recognize here one of the main intuitions of the Upanishads, and before them of the Rig-Veda:
> The Purusha is all,
> What has been, what will be;
> He is the Lord of immortality. (*Rig Veda,* 10.90.2).

The Purusha of the size of a thumb
rests in the middle of the self . . . .
like a light without smoke,
Lord of what has been and what will be.
He indeed is today;
He indeed shall be tomorrow! (*Katha Upanishad,* 4.12-13)

(We are inevitably reminded of the phrase in the Letter to the Hebrews 13.8; cp. Rev. 1.4, 8, etc.: "Christ is the same yesterday and today and for ever").

Lord of all, Knower of all,
the Inner Controller, the Source of all,
the Beginning and the End of all that is created.

(*Mandukya Upanishad,* 6)

(cp. "I am the Alpha and the Omega, the Beginning and the End" of Rev. 21.6).

He alone is All,
All that has been, all that will be
He is the Eternal!
Knowing him, one overcomes death;
No other path is there for release! (*Kaivalya Upanishad,* 9)

2. The ways in which those mystics formulate their experience may seem to have little in common with the general approach of Christian theology. However, in assessing them no one should forget the equally great difficulty found by so many Christian mystics also when they attempt to describe their own experiences, and the suspicions which hung on even the greatest of them. Furthermore the encounter of Christian thought with mystical and theological formulations which in no way depend on the Semitic and Greek mental categories on which Christian theology is based, cannot fail to be extremely enriching.

3. Many texts of Vatican II could be quoted to illustrate this statement; e.g.:

All the faithful, whatever their condition or state, are called by the Lord, each in his own way, to that perfect holiness whereby the Father himself is perfect (*Lumen Gentium,* 11, in *The Documents of Vatican II;* tr. W. M. Abbott, p. 29).

71

All the faithful of Christ of whatever rank or status are called to the fulness of the Christian life and to the perfection of charity (ibid., 40, op. cit., p. 67).

As those who lead others to perfection, bishops should be diligent in fostering holiness among their clerics, religious, and laity according to the special vocation of each (*Christus Dominus* 15, op. cit., p. 407).

4. *Sannyasa:* the life of renunciation according to Hindu tradition. *Sannyasi:* one who has renounced the world (cp. *sadhu, muni*).

5. (C.I.C. 487) Does not the Spirit here give us a hint that the eremitical life lies outside the scope of any institutionalization, and that the Law should be content merely to protect and safeguard it, without attempting to regulate it? It is as if the eremitical life fulfils the function in the Church of being a standing reminder that the Spirit is sovereignly free and is bound to no forms whatsoever.

6 The Carthusian Order: named after La Chartreuse, France; founded in the eleventh century by St Bruno, in which the monks live a partly hermit life.

7. Carmelite Order: an Order originally of hermits, which first appeared in Palestine in the thirteenth century and was later introduced into the West, becoming one of the Mendicant Orders. St John of the Cross and St Teresa of Avila are among the greatest members of the Order.

8. Hesychasm is a spiritual movement which developed in the Eastern Church during the medieval period in close connection with the contemplative tradition of the Fathers of the Desert. The name comes from the Greek *hesuchia,* which means quietness, silence, solitude. The role of the Hesychasts in the spreading of Jesus' prayer will be referred to later on. As for the methods of concentration and breath-control of the school, they are not without analogy to the Hindu yoga.

9. A letter plus allocution of Pope Paul VI *to the* Trappists is worth quoting here (see *Documentation Catholique,* Paris, 4-18 May 1969):

Your apostolate is the hidden life itself, and your mission is to uphold the contemplative life and to witness to it anew in our times . . . . Silence is a most precious inheritance of your Order and retains its full value even now. . . . Speak to the world by your silence. The monk looks only at God, desires only God, is attached to God alone, but his contemplation benefits the whole Church. The Church is indeed in need of it in order to maintain and develop her own life. The Church needs souls with a rich inner life, devoted to recollecting themselves in God. If there is a scarcity of these, the whole Mystical Body will suffer and be impoverished. Mystical contemplation keeps alive in the Church the knowledge of God which depends on experience, and without which the understanding of the Word of God will lack a necessary dimension. If the souls of the faithful are not to wither, they need to be refreshed with the living water which springs up in the heart of contemplatives. Not everyone accepts your witness: the contemplative life is too near to the mystery of God to be understood by the world. Do not seek to be understood by men at all costs. Be simply yourselves. God himself will see to it that your light shines. Your pastoral task is your hidden life.

CHAPTER 6

1. Any prayer which, even unconsciously, treats God as an *object* cannot be a real prayer in spirit and in truth. God cannot, strictly speaking, be an object, since the "object" essentially depends on the subject who "puts it before" himself (*ob-jicit*). One cannot properly speak of God in the third person, even if linguistic conventions can scarcely avoid doing so. God comes first. *I* am only in the *Thou* which God says to me. God alone is in the first person. If it is to be true, our inner experience of God should be of him as a first person, the one and only *I*. As long as we try to reach God by forming concepts of him and thereby making him an object, we cannot find him. He is only to be found in the experience of my own *I*, which is a participation (and not an outward projection) of the *I* of God. Yet the mystery of the *I-Thou* within the uniqueness of the essential *I* still remains. This is the whole mystery of the Holy Trinity in which man participates by the very fact of his creation and into whose fulness he is taken up by the grace of the divine adoption (cp. John 1.12; Rom. 8.14ff).

CHAPTER 7

1. *Yoga* (from *yug,* union): exercises of various kinds, designed
to help the mind to concentrate. *Yoga* includes preparatory
physical exercises like *asana* (postures) and *pranayama* (control
of breathing). The essence of the yogic method is *ekagrata,*
or concentration of the mind upon a point, which gives
mastery over the flow of mental images and detachment from
external or internal sensations and perceptions. This concentration may be focused upon a sound, a physical or imaginary
point, or a stylized image (of the *guru,* for example). A simple
but effective method is to fix the whole attention on the
breathing process. It is also important that the body be erect
and that the inner image on which concentration is focused
be placed in one of the *cakras* (see below) in the axis of the
body. The final aim is to discover oneself in the hidden depth
of the *guha* (see below); beyond the plane of passing phenomena, whether external or internal.

   The expression "Christian *yoga*", though often used in these
days, is nevertheless confusing. There is no such thing as a
specifically "Christian" *yoga,* any more than there is Christian logic or Christian gymnastics. Of course anyone can make
use of some elements of traditional *yoga* for his own spiritual
training, and can do this in a Christian context. He can even
intersperse yogic exercises with Christian *mantras* (possibly
in place of Hindu ones, though these are never strictly pre-
scribed); but none of this is sufficient to justify its being
termed "Christian". *Yoga* in itself aims at arresting the mental
process of forming ideas, and then at the total disappearance
of all images whatever, including even inner verbalization,
whether they be Hindu, Buddhist, or Christian. The real
question is: How can an authentic and integral *yoga* help the
Christian to deepen his prayer and his experience of God?
This in fact is precisely what we have been seeking throughout
this book, although we have started from premisses different
from those of *yoga* proper.

2. We speak here of *shakti* in its primitive meaning, without
reference to later speculations or mythology.

3. Self-awareness, or experience of the self, underlies all our
psychological life, but cannot be restricted to, or identified
with, any of our psychological activities, either of the intellect

or of the will. In ordinary psychological experience the awareness of ourselves is always mixed with our perception of things,
whether these belong to the external world or to our bodies,
or to the sphere of our mind (thought and imagination).
All such knowledge is transient, and we are very well aware
that in the very core of ourselves we transcend it and that
through all the changing events and circumstances of our life,
both external and internal, we ourselves remain the same, un-
altered and intact. Furthermore, in deep sleep, when we are
not even dreaming, we seem quite unconscious of ourselves
and yet we still *are* (exist). The experience of self-awareness
is to be simply conscious of oneself without any qualification
whatever; to be aware of simply being, apart from any kind
or mode of being, apart from any consciousness of being one
who does this or that. Our consciousness is reduced to its
central point, as in deep sleep, but at the same time we are as
fully aware as in our waking state. (It is an open question
whether this consciousness of simply being includes the consciousness of being distinct from other beings, above all from
the Absolute Being. Indian tradition generally answers in the
negative; *advaita,* non-duality, is the essence of that supreme
experience; and this is difficult to refute. Yet this is just the
point where the experience of Jesus comes in to solve the
paradox of advaitic experience, and through the revelation of
the trinitarian mystery confirms the faith of those who believe
in the reality of their personality and of the universe as a
whole.)

There is no doubt that it is in the experience of self-
awareness that man reaches the highest point of his psychological life. That experience is the natural substratum of any
authentic mystical experience. At other levels of psychological
life the mystery of God is apprehended only through concepts
and images, all of them mere symbols, essentially incomplete
and for ever incapable of leading man to the final goal which
is written into his nature (cp. Aquinas, *Summa Theol.* I-II,
Questions 1-5, treating of the end of man's existence; also *Pars*
I, *Question* 12, on the Vision of God). Only at the very centre
of his being can man have a real glimpse of the central mystery
of God.

The aim of all *yoga* (union) is to attain to this point. Until
that is reached, God is imagined, conceived, and understood

as *other,* as a projection of the otherness of creatures. This does justice neither to the otherness between God and us nor to his mysterious immanence in the core of our souls. But then God is experienced in one's coincidence with one's self beyond all *vritti* (movements) of the mind, in the self's indivisible centre. It is really the experience of the silence of the Father, of the unmanifested mystery of the Godhead, before (as it were) the Father calls the Son, and all of us in the Son, by that "Thou" which fills time and eternity.

Some thinkers prophesy that the evolution of humankind is tending towards the generalization of this experience among men. Man was first *homo faber,* then *homo sapiens.* In the last millennium before Christ man reached the age of philosophy, that is, he began to reflect on his own act of thinking. (This happened at the same time in Greece, India, and China, the three foremost areas of human development.) And now we see signs that man can no longer be satisfied with myths, or even with the intellectual concepts which until recently have been his pride. Herein lies the tragic situation of all religions today, Christianity not excepted. In the frightening whirl of contemporary evolution the only point on which a man can stand without being constantly in danger of losing his foothold and being washed away no one knows where, is that very central and fundamental experience. Religion is in the same predicament too. As regards the Church in particular, however praiseworthy may be her recent endeavour to reform herself and to keep abreast of the world and the present mentality of man, this by itself is not enough. She must aim at nothing less than to guide more and more of her children through and beyond symbols to that very central point where the Spirit abides within the spirit of man (Rom. 8.16).

4. We refer here to the Scholastic interpretation of the "gifts of the Holy Spirit". According to the medieval Latin doctors, man's capacities and his natural virtues, even when elevated by grace, are unable to raise the (Christian) believer to the divine level of activity which is expected of him as a child of God. In a man transformed by grace there must therefore be certain "passivities" in his faculties, both of knowledge and action which can only be the result of a higher, more direct, and more divine influence of the Holy Spirit. Such are the seven traditional "gifts" of the Holy Spirit—wisdom and

understanding, counsel and might, knowledge, godliness, and holy fear.

The Spirit then works within the level of man's faculties, in order to help him to live his life as a son of God in time and space according to the changing circumstances of his earthly pilgrimage. His work in the soul becomes more and more powerful according as the faculties in which he operates are higher and more subtle. But his operation in, and possession of, the soul reach their climax when a man has at last made contact with the highest point or centre of himself, when he has transcended all his limitations and already participates mystically in the condition which is his in the eternity of God.

5. *Vedanta* (*Veda-anta:* the end of the Veda), that is, the teaching of the Upanishads, and in a specialized use, the system of philosophy which expounds this teaching.

6. "*Neti, neti*" ("Not this, not that"): an expression which recurs as a kind of refrain in the *Brihad-aranyaka Upanishad* (e.g., 4.2.4) and means that the Absolute is beyond anything which can be thought or spoken. It is in the Hindu tradition the equivalent of Christian apophatism.

7. *Dark Night* (E. Allison Peers) 3, 4

CHAPTER 8

1. The holy (or Divine) Office consists of the prayers (Psalms, Scripture readings, hymns) which clerics have to perform either in common or privately at specified hours of the day.

2. Compare *Hindu-Christian Meeting Point,* pp. 9ff. (Please note that chapters 2 and 3 have been inverted.)

3. Canons: bodies of ecclesiastics (founded in the Middle Ages) who are specially responsible for the celebration of the Liturgy, either in cathedrals (secular canons) or in monasteries (regular canons). Benedictines are monks who follow the Rule of St Benedict (sixth century).

CHAPTER 9

1. *Namajapa,* from *nama,* name, and *japa,* prayer (especially the almost inaudible repetition of *mantras*).

2. *Mantra:* specifically: Vedic hymn or sacrificial formula; generally: a formula of prayer.

3. Is expressed most beautifully in the Roman collect for the 10th Sunday after Pentecost (old missal).

4. "Let the remembrance of Jesus be present in every breath you draw, and you will discover the value of the solitary life."

5. *Mount Athos.* A famous peninsula in Northern Greece, which has been inhabited only by monks for the past thousand years. On *Hesychasm,* see above, chapter 5, note 8.

6. The best introduction to this form of prayer remains the book *The Way of a Pilgrim* (translated from the Russian by R. M. French, S.P.C.K. 1963). See also *Writings from the Philokalia on the Prayer of the Heart* (translated by Kadloubovsky and Palmer, Faber 1951).

7. *Trisagion:* the "Holy, Holy, Holy" which Isaiah heard sung by the seraphim before the throne of Yahweh and which is incorporated into all Christian liturgies.

8. *Guha:* see, for example:

> Hard to see, deep hidden in the depth,
> set in the cave, abyss-dweller,
> primordial . . .
> More subtle than the subtle
> greater than the great,
> hidden in the cave of a creature here
> is the Atman . . .
> The inner Self of all things,
> the only Master (*Katha Upanishad,* 2.12; 2.20; 5.12).

> The Person (*Purusha*) himself is everything here . . .
> He who knows That, set in the secret place (*guha*)—
> He here on earth my friend, rends asunder the knot of
> ignorance.
> Vast, heavenly, of unthinkable form,
> And more minute than the minute, It shines forth.
> It is further than the far, yet here near at hand,
> Set down in the secret place (*guha*)
> Even here among those who behold (It).
>
> (*Mundaka Upanishad,* 2.1.10; 3.1.7)

OM! He who knows Brahman attains the highest!

He who knows Brahman as the Real, as Knowledge, as the Infinite,

Set down in the secret place (*guha*) and in the highest heaven.
                                        (*Taittiriya Upanishad*, 2.1)

9. *Brahman:* the Absolute, the Supreme Being.

10. *Atman:* the soul, the inner Self, as opposed to the *ego*.

11. Compare these aphorisms of Evagrios:

    It is not because thou hast reached indifference that thou shalt pray in truth, for one can remain among thoughts, however simple, yet be busy with them, and hence be far from God (55).

    Do not picture God within thee in thy prayer, nor let thy intellect be impressed with any form; but formless go to him who has no form (66).

    When thou shalt have passed in thy prayer beyond all bliss, then in truth shalt thou have found prayer (153).

12. The Greek Fathers delighted in contemplating the Father as the Source, "Source of the Godhead", "Source of all that is". Compare this saying of Sri Ramana Maharishi: "To disappear in the Source, that is truly (the aim, *or* the essence of) *karma* and *bhakti* (action and devotion), (of) *yoga* and *jnana* (wisdom) (*Upadesa saram*, 10)".

CHAPTER 10

1. The Tirukkural is one of the most important books in Tamil literature, dating probably from before the Christian era.

2. The "A" sound is the indeterminate "a", as in English "among": the "U" is pronounced like the vowel in the English word "book".

3. All the Vedas announce that *Word*,
    all the penances proclaim it . . .
    That word in short I shall tell you;
    that is OM!
    This, Brahman, imperishable, it is;
    This, the Beyond, imperishable it is!

That is the best foundation,
that is the supreme one (*Katha Upanishad*, 2. 15-17).

The bow is OM, the arrow the self;
Brahman the target.
By a mind undistracted it has to be pierced,
One becoming "That" (*Mundaka Upanishad*, 2.2.4).

Fixed in OM the wise man attains That,
tranquil, unaging, deathless, supreme!
(*Prasna Upanishad*, 5.7)

OM! This syllable is all this:
What was, what is, what will be—
everything is just OM!
And whatever may transcend the three times,
that too is just OM! (*Mandukya Upanishad*, 1).

Rig is speech; *Soman, breath* . . .
that is a couple:
Vag and *Prana* (speech and breath)
Rig and *Saman;*
they are joined together in OM!
(*Chandogya Upanishad*, 1.1.5-6)

There are really two *Brahman* to be known,
Brahman which is sound
and Brahman which is beyond sound.
Non-sound is revealed by sound.
OM is the Brahma-sound;
going through it, one attains the non-sound . . .
As a spider climbs by its thread to free space,
so through OM the knower reaches freedom . . .
He crosses over with OM as his raft
to the other side of space of the heart,
in the inner space,
into the hall of Brahman (*Maitri Upanishad*, 6. 22. 28).

4.   More even than the Hindu *sannyasin,* the Christian monk
is invited by a divine call to concentrate his mind and
heart (not exclusively but primarily) beyond the mysteries
of Creation, Incarnation and Redemption themselves—on
the very mystery of God, the Blessed Trinity. But for the
enlightened *sannyasin,* the ultimate simplicity of the
Absolute can rightly be named by reduplication *sat,* being,
cit, thought, *ananda,* bliss, knowing as he does that the

Deity has not, but is, by essence, Existence, Intelligence, and Beatitude. Repeating that sacred formula *saccidananda*, the Christian gives it a new and mysterious meaning, unknown to man, because such knowledge is above any created intelligence, but was communicated (*in novissimo tempore*) to all mankind through ultimate revelation by the Word made flesh. And more fervently and with greater appreciation than any of his fellow-sannyâsins, can the Christian monk utter: SAT, when thinking of the Father, the principleless Principle, the very source and end of the expansion and "recollection" of the divine Life; CIT, when remembering the eternal Son, the Logos, the intellectual consubstantial Image of the Existent; ANANDA, when meditating on the Paraclete, unifying together the Father and the Son. And just as AUM is one sound from three elements (A,U,M), so also the mystery of the one identical Essence in three "hypostases" may be expressed by that pregnant sacred utterance. It rings like the symbol of the silent Deity (J. Monchanin).

5. Would that I were many! (*Chandogya Upanishad*, 6.2).